The Lady
with the Crown

Applause for The Lady with the Crown

Tragic and uplifting, hopeless and hopeful, heartwarming and heartbreaking—Kathleen Canrinus's memoir of life before and after her mother's devastating brain injury is a testament to the physical and psychological indomitability of them both. It is a story that everyone, especially physicians, families, and patients dealing with irreversible neurological dysfunction, should be required to read because of its gritty, matter-of-fact account of tragedy and how to make it a beginning and not an end.

David B. Teplow, Professor of Neurology
David Geffen School of Medicine at UCLA

Kathleen Canrinus has at last broken the silence and delivered the absorbing story of her mother and herself. Decades of close observation feed a narrative that tumbles forward with poignant surprises, building to unexpected triumph. Heartbreaking and hilarious, Canrinus's well-crafted memoir is an inspiring and satisfying read.

Sylvia E. Halloran, poet, editor,
author of *The Ballad of Billy Shay*

Writing with sensitivity and compassion, Kathleen Canrinus dives deep into a remarkable bittersweet journey that depicts a complex mother-daughter relationship. It is a story of "strengths and endurance" in the author's words. With tenderness and humor she explores her competing emotions when as a teenager she and her mother reverse roles in a saga that spans more than 50 years. If you've ever had to deal with the pain associated with a family member's sudden disability, this book is for you.

Francine Toder, Ph.D., Psychologist
Inward Traveler: 51 Ways to Explore the World Mindfully

This memoir draws a portrait of mother-daughter love, each chapter arriving at observations and insights quiet and miraculous as the path moonshine creates on water. Kathleen Canrinus offers us a story about frustration and sorrow, treasuring, and the soul-rewarding capacity to give one's all.

Sheila Bender, memoirist and poet,
A New Theology: Turning to Poetry in a Time of Grief;
Since Then: Poems and Short Prose.

The Lady
with the Crown

A Story of Resilience

Kathleen Canrinus

Ashland, Oregon

Book design by Ray Rhamey

Print edition ISBN 978-1-7330344-7-0

Library of Congress Control Number:

Contents

For my mother and father
and brother—
and our families

Acknowledgments

For their helpfulness and support, thank you to Molly Best Tinsley, teacher, editor, advocate; Kathryn Maller, friend, writer, and writing partner, and Sylvia Halloran, writer and workshop facilitator. Over thirteen years, members of various writing groups have also read and responded to the stories about my mother that became *The Lady in the Crown*. My husband endured and adapted to the demands of my writing life. It took a village. Thank you, all.

Preface

Over my lifetime, I have met high-achieving people with careers that brought them recognition and others with great talent or wealth. Someday, biographers might write about them—their family histories, their setbacks, and finally their extraordinary accomplishments.

My mother, on the other hand, will leave no enduring mark on the world. She has lived most of her life in anonymity—her world small, her odds of survival poor and once overcome, her odds of a long and happy life even poorer. Yet she finds joy. I am the witness to her achievement and also its beneficiary. I am the keeper of memories. It fell to me to share the story of the events that shaped us both.

1954

Hamburger Saturdays

Saturdays, we had burgers for lunch—fried
and served between slices of soft wheat bread
with Best Foods mayonnaise and ketchup and
a leaf of iceberg lettuce—on matching Mel-
mac dishes at a hand-me-down sunny yellow
table with curved chrome legs—Formica like
the counter at Sammy Locastro's diner where
we showed up every blue moon for homestyle
dinners on thick oval plates—Sammy for
company, and no clean-up after.

All those hamburger Saturdays—the
wooden napkin holder my brother made in
shop class, the same glass salt and pepper
shakers, the black linoleum with whorls of
white, and sharp-eyed wallpaper roosters—
watching. I'm watching too. The four of us,
points of a compass. My brother and I, the
East and West to our parents' solid North and
South. A stable circle. Held in place by time.
Fixed by gravity. Oriented. Centered. Upright.
Unsuspecting.

Part 1

Other things may change us, but we start and
end with the family.

Anthony Brandt

Chapter 1
Hurry up. Now!

When I was a girl, my mother talked to everyone. If laughter is a measure, she connected as easily with bank and grocery store clerks, gas station attendants, or any stranger in a line next to her, as she did with the droves of people she knew.

From age two through college and her first jobs—even after she married and had me—my mother lived with her grandmother in a tiny stucco house. So naturally, on trips to town, my mother might bump into a classmate from kindergarten, one of her high school students, the parent of a nursery school child she had taught, or a Latvian immigrant from her night school English classes. When the encounter was with a friend of her grandmother's, conversations took place in a dialect spoken in the Piedmont region of Italy where our family and most Italian immigrants in Los Gatos came from.

Whatever the language, there Mom would be, her white blouse coming untucked from her pedal pushers, her wavy brown hair unbound, her hands in constant motion—arms too—her gestures growing larger toward the climax of one of her stories, her head turning this way and that as if the action was taking place right there in the moment. And all the while, my brother and I stood waiting, impatient hostages—embarrassed and a little jealous too. Her world was big, and we were an important part of it but not all of it.

As our mother, she did everything she could to make our world big too. Like other kids in the new neighborhood, we had dogs and cats and the resulting puppies and kittens. We also made homes for rats and parakeets, and goldfish. Once, our mother even borrowed a caged skunk from a local museum that lent live animals, her way of teaching us about wild critters. She took us to an observatory to see Mars when it orbited close to the earth, to San Francisco to see *Wheatfields* and other Van Gogh paintings and foreign films like *Mr. Hulot's Holiday*. We also heard Yehudi Menuhin play violin.

Still, I had only the vaguest notion then that our mother was not like other mothers in spite of the evidence. She wore pants, not dresses, went to work, and welcomed our friends anytime, without a phone call first. She hosted overnights on our lawn, offered army surplus blankets and card tables for tent-making in or out of the house, cleared the garage one summer for our pretend circus, and served pancake dinners on Friday nights. Summers, when my brother Mike and I tired of picking the prune crop in our neighbor's orchard, Mom got down on her hands and knees and picked too—a bucket for Mike then a bucket for me—and like us, batted at the yellow jackets buzzing around overripe fruit that lay on the ground. But on the hottest of summer days, she'd yell down to the orchard, "Quick. Change into your swimsuits and get in the car. I'll help you tomorrow. Hurry! Let's go to the beach. Now!"

When so summoned, Mike and I unpinned our knee pads from our jeans and abandoned our buckets. "Last one home's a rotten egg," I'd yell, and take off for the house. While we changed into our suits, Mom slapped together peanut butter and jelly sandwiches and a smelly one for herself—cheese or liverwurst with a thick slice of onion.

"Can't we go to a pool instead?" I asked. I didn't like sand in my food or in my mouth after getting knocked over by cold salty waves, and the backs of my knees stung for days from sunburn.

"We're going to the beach. Hurry. Get in the car," she called from the kitchen. "And don't forget the suntan lotion."

As to why our mother was always in such a rush, I never asked. I don't believe that at some level, she knew how her life would change before its midpoint. It was simply one of those mysteries—just the way it was. Caught up in the whirlwind of her energy, my brother and I clambered into the back seat where Mom had already toted towels in a drawstring swim bag and a picnic that included Ball jars with Kool Aid. She positioned these on the floor near our feet and in our charge.

"Sea & Ski," she reminded us as we pulled out of the driveway. We finished slathering on the pale green lotion—though it never really worked—before the first long curve in the uphill stretch of highway over the summit and down to the beach.

No toys, no shovels, pails, or balls. No blankets, ice chests, or umbrellas. No chairs, no hats. No advance notice. Sand and shells, seaweed and waves were enough.

Sometimes, our friends came too; anyone who could get permission and arrive in time was welcome. Other times, Mom invited a friend of hers—adults up front, boys and girls squeezed into the back seat, bare skin to bare skin, sweaty legs and arms stuck together for the forty-minute ride. As soon as the key turned in the ignition, the conversation in the front seat started up. By the time the car shifted into high gear, so had the grown-ups' chatter about school board decisions and elections, evening meetings, teachers, new hires, curriculum. With one hand on the steering wheel, the other in motion to emphasize this or that point, Mom raced along the highway she knew by heart at speeds synchronized to the flow of words. I paid little attention. In those days, I had only two passions, reading and horses. But occasionally, I overheard a whispered "nervous breakdown" or "divorce," references to the complexity and unpredictability of adult life that caused the only hairline cracks in the rock-solid years of my childhood.

When it was just the three of us on a beach trip, our mother found a spot near the water, stripped to her skirted suit, and planted herself—knees bent, heels dug in, and bare feet resting against mounds of damp sand, as against dual accelerators. Although she had been a lifeguard and long-distance swimmer in her youth, she didn't enter the water. Her head wrapped in a towel, turban-style, she never took her eyes off us as we played, never flagged in her vigilance while the waves beat their rhythms on the shore and hissed back to sea.

When she decided we'd had enough, we left. As soon as we were on the highway, my brother and I started up. "Please, stop at the juice stand. Please, please." Tired, with our sandy bottoms shifting uncomfortably on damp towels, and me wishing again we had just gone to a pool, my brother and I were prepared to whine the whole long, hot thirsty ride home. Very occasionally, she pulled off at the All You Can Drink and rushed us out of the car. "Here's a dime. Take your pick. Cherry, orange, grape, or apple." If we hesitated at all, she ordered apple for us.

But in general, my mother was incapable of taking longer than she absolutely needed to do anything, incapable of ever slowing the snappy pace at which she moved through a day, the exception being when she ran into someone she knew. And once she finally finished talking, she rushed us on to whatever was next. "Quick! Hop in the car." And off we'd go.

Chapter 2
The Luck of the Draw

Until the Christmas I was ten, I had no sign my mother had anything but the happiest of childhoods. That year, my grand-mother had invited our family of four to San Francisco for Christmas dinner. Smiling and calling down greetings, she welcomed us to her upstairs flat from the landing where the carpeted stairs reversed directions. Scent of roasting turkey mixed with cigar hung in the stairwell and in the rooms above, masking the familiar moldy undertones of her fog-drenched flat.

After hugging us, our grandmother, who my brother and I called Nanny, marched us over to a tree so small it fit on top of her TV, packages piled on the living room floor nearby. Seated in his stuffed chair, my grandfather greeted us in gruff accent-ed English. Shuffling the soggy stump of his cigar from one side of his mouth to the other with his tongue, he urged us to open our presents.

From under folds of white tissue paper in a Macy's box, I pulled out a black wool tight skirt, the very gift I longed for, the skirt every girl I knew was wearing, the one my mother refused to buy for me.

My mother stared at the skirt and then at her mother. "Kathleen's too young to wear black," she said in an unfamiliar and disturbing tone. The tension in the room was palpable.

Even my ten-year-old self recognized that my mother's comment couldn't possibly have been entirely about the skirt. Nanny stood and crossed the living room to a window, opened it halfway, then left the room without saying anything. Confused and fighting back tears, I set the gift aside and took my father's suggestion to go play.

Mike followed me down the rickety back stairs to the garage that held not just "the machine," as my grandmother called her car, but an entire inventory of unusual items. Sliding onto the front seat of the silver Hudson, we dared each other to touch the pale segmented rattlesnake tails that our grandfather hung from the rearview mirror. Next, we ran our hands over the sleek polished speedboat that our uncle had built and stored in a far corner of the garage. Neat rows of antlers spanned a nearby wall opposite a wall covered with license plates dating from the twenties. Molds shaped like castles, fish, and shells hung from hooks near a cupboard filled with homemade jams and marmalade. Fascinated by this orderly unchanging space unlike any at home, we explored until summoned to dinner.

Nothing unusual occurred during the meal, but as our family left the flat later, my father—a man of few words—leaned toward me. "*Your* mother hasn't forgiven *her* mother," he said. "I've talked to her, but she won't."

I knew my mother had grown up with her grandmother, not her mother. But until five years after the Christmas episode when my mother stopped speaking to her mother, I was unaware of the poor cards she was dealt from the start, the source of her festering resentment.

Chapter 3
Four Generations, One House

Of my family's history before my mother was born, I know that my great grandfather immigrated to Los Gatos, a small town in Northern California, during the Depression of the late 1800s. Tucked at the foot of the Coast Range with the Jesuit Novitiate and vineyards on the hillside above, Los Gatos resembled the grape-growing region he left behind in the rolling foothills of the Italian Alps.

I know that he and his older sons worked in the Novitiate vineyards until they earned enough money to buy a house on College Avenue and send for the rest of the family, and that with a few possessions in a steamer trunk, my Italian great grandmother arrived there in 1903 with her three younger children, my grandmother the youngest. She was five when she sailed to America, her only lasting memory of the country where she was born, the gold stars on the pale blue ceiling of the village church.

Gram—as I called my great grandmother—planted her salata, tomatoes, and other vegetables in the front yard between the camellias that lined the front of her two-bedroom home and the thorny hedge along the street. In the backyard, the barest trickle of a creek flowed from the hillside vineyards. It meandered across the property, carving miniature sand beaches from its banks before disappearing into a jumble of brush beneath a stand of eucalyptus. Near the chicken coop, flowers grew willy-nilly—towering pink hollyhocks, swaths of Jupiter's Beard, and clumps of daffodils in spring. In this setting, under the loving eye of my great grandmother, first my grandmother, then my mother, and finally I grew up.

Lined by a rock wall, a gravel path under a grape arbor connected the house to the garage and apartment above it. As a little girl, my grandmother watched her father build those rock walls and the arbor and plant the vines. My young mother watched her uncle Vincent harvest the grapes he then crushed in an enormous wooden barrel in the basement. When I dream myself back to the wine-sour air under the house, the ghostly shapes of my mother and grandmother appear at my side.

The grape arbor turns up again and again in frayed photos. My teenage grandmother in thick stockings and a dress. Gram in her long black coat with the fur collar, unsmiling. She never smiled in photos. My mother at age two in shorts, me at the same age wearing overalls. My brother, born a year after the end of WWII, on a tricycle.

In my earliest memory—with its faint foreshadowing of hospitals and caregiving—I'm squatting on the gravel path. On top of one wall, I've arranged small matchboxes and tiny squares of pink fabric cut from the blanket on my bed with toenail scissors—a hospital for half a dozen potato bugs, most of them injured during capture. Several are missing limbs but manage to scramble out from under their covers anyway. It's all I can do to keep my six-legged patients in their beds, so I don't hear my mother calling that it's time to come indoors.

After my brother arrived, our family of four moved out of Gram's house to the apartment above the garage. Turned loose every day to play outdoors, I headed down the gravel path to Gram's, but once I was older, I moved on to visiting places of interest in the yard with my friend Ricky from across the street. My mother had once found us naked in the creek, our clothes strewn along the bank. "Stay in the yard," she always reminded us, "and away from the creek." But what lay beyond it beckoned, and eventually, Ricky and I began to roam.

At first, we visited neighbors. But one day when my mother was busy with Gram—sometimes she even slept at Gram's— Ricky and I climbed to the flume that brought water to town from the mountains, another of my mother's forbidden destinations. We found sticks and poked drowned bugs in the gutter that ran under the covered half-pipe. We looked for a way to climb up on it too but weren't successful. So we trudged back down the hillside kicking dirt clods ahead of us. Ricky's mother spotted us first from where she was hanging clothes to dry and called to him to come home that instant.

As I passed our mailbox, I noticed my mother on Gram's front porch talking softly to a strange man in a suit who held a black bag. Near the camellia bush beside Gram's front door, other dark-clad figures whispered to each other. Something big had happened, but I didn't know what. Was I in trouble? Had my mother spotted Ricky and me too? When she saw me, she waved me off, and I scurried over to the chicken coop, where she soon joined me. Bending down to my eye level, she said very softly, "Gram is gone."

I didn't cry. I didn't know what she was talking about.

Not long after Gram's death, my parents took to sitting at the kitchen table after dinner. Mostly Mom talked, and she said "money" a lot. Neither she nor my father smiled when I galloped by on my stick horse or paid any attention to Mike when he turned somersaults on the floor next to them, his new trick. Something was up.

Chapter 4
Moving Up

My mother hefted me off the running board of our old Ford pickup. "Too cold to ride in the back, Kathleen," she said, and herded three-year-old Mike and me toward the cab. My father slid behind the wheel and reached for the choke while I straddled the gear stick, and Mom and Mike squeezed together to avoid the springs poking through the ancient leather seat.

"Where we going?" Mike asked as we pulled out of the driveway onto College Avenue.

"Wait and see," Mom told him, as if he'd just asked her what was in the huge box that appeared under the Christmas tree.

"But where?" he repeated, now really curious.

She pressed her lips together and covered her mouth to keep from blurting out her surprise.

So this was no ordinary ride. Maybe it had something to do with my parents' long talks after dinner, none of which held any meaning for me. As the old truck bounced toward our destination, I watched through the floorboards for oil spots on the road.

Our first stop was one of the mansions on Glen Ridge Avenue, a street that overlooked Los Gatos. Dad motioned for me to stay put.

"Mrs. Kretsinger lives in that big house," Mom explained, rolling down her window. "She is very rich. She owns *pro*-per-ty."

Mom looked over our heads at Dad. "Aren't we lucky, Fred? Tell Mrs. Kretsinger I'll send photos of construction."

"Be right back," he said and headed up the circular drive.

I scooted behind the wheel and reached toward the choke just like Dad, then grabbed the wheel and pretended to drive. I knew "right back" didn't really mean "right back."

"Where are you going?" Mom asked, playing along.

"To Uncle Vincent's," I said.

"Would you please pull over here first?" she said.

I mimed setting the emergency brake, and we watched my father ring the doorbell, hand an envelope to the old lady who answered, and exchange a few words with her.

Dad lifted me aside as he climbed back into the cab. "All set, Sweet Love," he said, winking at my mother.

"I can hardly believe it," she said. "We own a lot!"

"And not just any lot. It's the one you dreamed of," my father added.

Something significant had just happened. I knew this, but my mother's dreams lay beyond the scope of my interests. "Are we going home now?" I asked.

"Not yet," my mother said, "but not far away."

Ridgecrest Avenue curved up into the hills, crossing a creek near a grove of eucalyptus. We drove along the creek and on past orchards where mustard bloomed bright yellow under canopies of white blossoms. A little farther up the road, my father slowed the truck and shifted into first gear to make the sharp left turn onto a steep dirt driveway. It led to a field of meadow grasses with a stand of redwoods in an uphill corner.

"We're going to build our new house here," my mother beamed.

My brother and I scrambled out of the truck and ran toward the redwoods. I swung up on a branch of the tallest tree while Mike climbed one of the younger ones. From my perch, I saw that the bare ground at the center of the circle of trees would make a perfect hideout. I made my hands into binoculars and spied on my parents. They stood in the middle of the meadow a little apart, Mom facing one direction then another and holding her arms like a frame for what she saw in front of her.

Many years passed before I came to appreciate a view but never quite as much as my mother. A view was her highest priority and why she fell in love with the property after my father discovered it. He taught drivers ed after school to supplement his income. And now it had paid off beyond measure.

To design the house, my parents hired an architect and Lester Hopping, a carpenter, to help build it. During Dad's summer break from teaching, he worked alongside Lester. My mother complained with a laugh that every time she picked up a hammer or a saw or board or got up on the roof to help, either my brother or I had to go to the bathroom.

For most of my life, the Ridgecrest house was simply the place where I spent my childhood and adolescence. But in the process of re-imagining it now, I sense my mother's touches everywhere. Built on the side of a gently sloping hill, the L-shaped structure remained hidden until the steep driveway looped back on itself. Situated toward the rear of the property, single-story with redwood siding and a shake roof, the house blended into its woodsy setting.

Mornings, the sun shone on the front of the house, filling the rooms with light. Later, it dropped below the hills at the back, leaving views of colored clouds from the kitchen and dining area. The windows along the inside of the L overlooked the fertile Santa Clara Valley, then called The Valley of Heart's Delight, a patchwork of orchards extending east to the Diablo Range. In the other direction, framed in an enormous plate glass window, Mount Umunhum rose to its 3,400-foot height. I found out years later that my mother had hiked it many times as a girl. This view of one of the highest peaks in the Santa Cruz Mountains with grass, flowers, and our two Japanese maples in the foreground turned the sunken living room into the most dramatic realization of my mother's impulse to bring the outdoors in.

The entryway just inside the front door overlooked the living room where built-in bookshelves framed a red brick fireplace. Above them, matching driftwood grey wood paneling extended to the roof line. The mantle ran the width of the room, a perfect spot for displaying ceramic art made by friends and my father's golf trophies.

The kitchen was finished with black linoleum and wallpaper. This would have been my mother's choice—black was practical. It wouldn't show the dirt. And my father, caring only about his wife's happiness, held no opinions about the space he lived in as long as it was warm in winter. This last requirement perhaps accounts for the most unusual feature of the house. Between the beams of the living room's vaulted ceiling were exposed panels of yellow-gold fiberglass insulation.

I used to wonder why in the world it had been left that way. Was it an experiment? Was leaving it exposed simply a touch of the unexpected that appealed to my mother? It always seemed a little outrageous to me, but the random event that upended our lives reduced the look of the living room ceiling to a non-issue.

Bringing the smells of the outdoors in guided my mother's decisions in the garden. The seasonal scent of daphne and jasmine hung in the patio area near the front door and wafted into the hall that ran the length of the house from the entryway to my parents' bedroom. Their windows looked toward both the valley and the redwoods. Mike's knotty-pine-paneled room and my painted one overlooked the backyard—my room no less thrilling for being plain. Unlike my windowless pass-through room on College Avenue, it actually had a door and even a closet! I spent many happy hours reading on my bed by the window—the companions to my reading life, the pink trumpet blooms of naked ladies that showed up in summer, almond blossoms in winter, robins and lemon blossoms in spring.

We moved into our new home a few nights before Christmas in 1950, the rooms mostly empty of furniture. Varnished oak floors glowed yellow, gold, and pink in the light of lamps set here and there on cardboard boxes. Before we settled for the night, my mother strolled from room to room, pausing in each space and sighing. My father opened and closed closet doors, checking for a proper fit. Mike and I ran and skidded up and down the hall in our socks. Sometimes in dreams, I see that floor again, how it appeared lit from within. A profound sense of well-being settles over me until I notice the dream house is perched high on a cliff, precariously cantilevered above a roiling ocean.

The timing of our move to 16290 Ridgecrest Avenue not long after Gram's death must have covered the hole she left in our lives. I don't remember missing her. I don't remember my mother or father talking about her. Gram had gone to heaven, but in little ways, she was still around. Her couch traveled with us to the new house, one of the throws she crocheted from old cotton stockings over the back of it. Mom moved the old Wedgewood gas and wood-burning stove on legs too. When Gram's friend Mrs. Donadei babysat, she fried polenta in Gram's pan and sang to us in Italian. As before, Mom took us to visit Mrs. Canavero, another of Gram's friends, in her dimly lit house that smelled of garlic. But she never took us back to the old house even though Uncle Vincent inherited it. She had moved on and up.

In our new neighborhood in the hills, Mom befriended the stockbroker's young second wife and the doctor's wife too. That we now lived in a comparatively simple house in an upscale neighborhood tickled her but did not go to her head. It amused her to be the improbable outsider and never occurred to her to hide the beat-up 1934 pickup or apologize for it. Warm and friendly, she soon knew everyone on the hill. But her closest friends remained those from College Avenue days.

As to the trajectory of her life, my mother remained content and comfortable, if not thrilled, with its direction. She encouraged my father to seek promotions, and she returned to college to do graduate work so she could get a higher-paying job. But ambitious is too strong a word to describe her. Mainly, she wanted a better life for her family, for her children. She already had the house of her dreams and every reason to think that other dreams were within reach.

Indeed, many came true—promotions, vacations, a new car. And so the fifties unfolded in predictable ways—days and years tuned to seasons, holidays, the liturgical and school calendars—wonderful times with the normal disappointments of any mother and daughter, ordinary times, like those fried hamburgers at Saturday lunch, that gleam so bright in memory they can only be described as times of grace, with my mother still center stage.

Chapter 5
Muddying the Water

Inklings of my mother's imperfections emerged the year it rained so much the water in the new reservoir rose above the spillway. By the time she drove Mike and me to see the over-flowing basin, rain had been falling for two weeks straight. Water the color of café au lait gushed into the concrete culvert and cascaded toward the creek bed below. Frightened, yet unable to turn away, we joined the crowd to watch. In 1954, events of this sort still drew onlookers. TVs were new to most families in town, ours not yet among them.

The rainfall that filled the reservoir also turned our backyard into an irresistible and near-infinite source of mud, and when the rain stopped, my mother, not a stickler for cleanliness, turned my brother and me out to play in it. I enticed him to join me in a game, and his natural sweetness kept him from saying no to opening a bakery specializing in mudpies. But his interest waned shortly after he lugged two boards onto sawhorses for shelves to display our goods, and he wandered off to retrieve toy tractors and trucks from the garage. Pies, cookies and cakes, ladyfingers, turnovers—I labored until the color of the sky matched the black of my hands and arms, racing against Mom's imminent summons.

Our mother, never patient, summoned us with a cowbell when we were out in the orchards or woods or a shout if we were closer. I had just shaped my 133rd mud creation when the back porch light snapped on, and Mom opened the door. She stepped out onto the concrete slab my father had poured where my brother and I had scratched our names and those of our cats and dogs.

"Michael Anthony and Kathleen Lucile Canrinus," she called. "Dinner is on the table."

Though obsessed with seeing how many pastries I could make, I knew not to dally even though dinner probably was not on the table yet.

At her first close look at us, Mom burst out laughing. Ordering me to stay put, she placed her hands on Mike's shoulders and guided him through the service porch to the nearby "boys' bathroom." Then leaving the back door open, she led me in the other direction, past the roast resting on the stove, and down the hall to the "girls' bathroom"—opening doors and insisting I extend my arms in front of me, palms up the entire way.

The warm water stung as it ran off my numb hands in a dark lumpy stream. It turned the white porcelain sink brown, then swirled down the drain until only a smattering of tiny pebbles remained. I wanted to stay at the sink until my hands warmed to normal, but Mom was ramping up her urgings, peppering them with her extensive vocabulary of Italian swear words and a few in English.

No sooner had I shut off the water than I heard shrieks and shouts and thuds coming from the kitchen. "Jesus Christo! Goddamnit!" Mom yelled. "Drop it."

I rushed to dry my hands and find out what the ruckus was about. Dad was standing near the kitchen table, his chair on its side, the evening paper scattered on the floor. My mother was poised near the oven holding a knife in the air. To my surprise, my brother's friend Dave was in the kitchen too, backing up, edging his way toward the service porch, his only escape route without confronting an enraged, red-faced Italian with a knife, as he later described her. And through the open door behind him, a flash of white and black disappeared up the path. Dave turned and followed in hot pursuit.

"That goddamned dog of his stole the roast," Mom said, "right off the stove."

Dad waited until she dropped the knife before speaking. "Let's go to Sammy's diner," he said.

Dave stayed away from our house for a couple of weeks. His mother, the doctor's wife, bought a replacement roast, and the incident passed into neighborhood legend. Dave's version was the best.

Even at Sammy's, school monopolized our dinner table conversations. How could it not with the director of the parent participation nursery school, the vice principal of the high school, and two students in the family? Usually, Mike and I checked in first. But after Sammy poured Mom and Dad's coffee, and we'd ordered our dinners, and Mom stopped cursing the dumb disobedient Dalmatian that stole our dinner, she launched into her day.

"The hardest part of the job is the mommies," she said, a refrain common to all teachers. "Lillian brought me her favorite books on child psychology today. She says I'll find them interesting."

"I had fun in the mud," my brother interjected.

Mom ignored him. "Lillian is very very smart," she said, in a tone reserved for the very rich as well. "Lillian has a Ph.D," emphasis on the D.

"Today, I made a hundred thirty-three pies," I said.

With her voice growing louder, Mom just stared at Dad and continued. "Does she think I'm not doing a good enough job, that I need more education?"

My father didn't respond.

Eyes on him, she waited. "Well?"

He reached for the pack of Chesterfields in his shirt pocket.

"Fred?" my mother said staring harder.

"What do you think?" he said and then paused. "Experience counts too, Dorothy. You know that."

Mom let the subject of her qualifications drop when Sammy delivered our dinners.

"Anyway, I invited a speaker to our next evening meeting, an expert in child development from Oakland," Mom said, cutting her meat.

"How do you think she'll go over with Lillian?" my father asked.

"That better depend on what she says, not the color of her skin," my mother snapped.

Dad waited a bit before speaking again and paused mid-sentence as if considering whether to finish. "I wonder if Lillian ever heard about...about what happened with Johnny?"

I knew what he was talking about. We all did.

My mother slapped the table. "It worked, didn't it? After I bit him, he stopped biting the other kids."

She put on her "I'm right" face, chin out, eyes open wide, lips shut tight.

Dad said nothing.

"At least his mother is talking to me again," Mom continued, "and didn't withdraw him. Besides, little Johnny had his revenge."

We all knew about this too. While she was talking to another mother one day, Johnny tied her shoelaces together—with the intended result.

"Johnny and I are even," she said, laughing. "That kid!"

In the brief lull after her laughter, Sammy dropped by our table. His son played Junior Varsity basketball, and Sammy wanted Dad's opinion on whether the team had a chance to take first place in the league.

So I never did get the opportunity to tell the story of my day in the mud, to brag about mudpies, an impressive number eleven shy of a dozen dozen. The number meant something to me. I had persevered until my hands turned to blocks of ice, and my task became more painful than fun. I would have liked to tell her about my accomplishment before the excitement wore off. Too soon, the rain would melt my creations into shapeless piles and smears and along with them that thrill. Instead, I sat quietly as Mom took over the dinnertime conversation, a disappointing but not life-changing occurrence.

An incident that did shift my relationship to her occurred during one of our family's card games. Besides listening to records or to the radio, playing cards was one of the ways we spent time together indoors. From years of games, only two stand out: the Saturday afternoon Mom taught me Russian Bank. Just me. And the game that changed our relationship.

On the first occasion, she found me reading on my bed and without telling me why, invited me to follow her to the living room. Something in her voice hinted at a surprise. She had set up the card table and put her beloved Strauss waltzes on the HiFi. "I just learned a new game. From Irmadelle." she said, referring to our neighbor, the stockbroker's wife. "Want to play?"

I hesitated. This was a game adults played.

"It's a little complicated, but I think you might like it. I'll teach you."

So I slid my skinny flat-chested self onto the chair opposite her while she patiently explained the rules. Next, she showed me how to play with our hands visible to each other, and then we played several real games—my mother nodding encouragingly when I hesitated or suggesting I rethink a play with a gentle question and praising me for how quickly I learned the rules.

No other time from childhood is bathed in the warm glow of this one—how flattered I was by her invitation to learn a new game, how grown up I felt, how pleased that she believed I could learn the game, how openly the affection flowed between us.

These feelings were soon turned upside-down during a high stakes game of Crazy Eights Mom, Mike, and I played after dinner. The loser had to do the dishes.

I was pondering what to discard when out of the corner of my eye, I noticed my mother sitting sideways on her chair and fumbling to close the junk drawer behind her. But not quickly enough. There, sticking out of the drawer, were several cards that matched the deck we were using, cards she was supposed to get rid of to win the game.

"Mom!" I said, confused and shocked. "That's cheating. You're cheating. I can't believe you'd cheat your own children!"

"I didn't want to do the dishes," she shot back. Not a hint of apology.

Cheating did not fit my picture of my mother. It had never occurred to me that she wouldn't play fair. She told us not to cheat. She sent us to catechism where we learned cheating was a sin and to mass and confession. From then on and way beyond the after-dinner card game itself, a cloud of disillusionment and distrust lent a suspicious edge to the intimacy of our ritual games.

Mom wasn't who I thought she was. She had flaws, and those flaws were about to multiply exponentially in the stormy times ahead.

Chapter 6
Breasts: Mom's and Mine

Mom's

When my mother took me to the dentist for the first time, I refused to let the man near me. His office smelled of licorice, and he was wearing a white coat like the doctor, who stuck me with needles while my mother held me down. Worse, the dentist spoke to me in a sing-song voice, faking that he was about to do something really nice, as in, "Sit right here, young lady. Your milkshake will be right up." But I knew better and wanted none of it. Flailing and sobbing and screeching, I balked. No way was I going to sit in that weird-looking chair with the torture tools.

Conceding defeat after a few minutes of cajoling, my embarrassed mother apologized to the dentist, not to me, as I thought she should, and hustled me out to the car. Same outcome when she tried again. And the third time too.

On one of her failed attempts, she must have mentioned that her own dentist once made a mold of her mouth to use as a model of perfect teeth. I can only imagine this reference to her straight, aligned, cavity-free teeth as a means of persuading me to cooperate. She truly wasn't vain.

Her perfect teeth, unlike the dayglow-white make-overs today's celebrities prefer, resembled those of a movie star from the 40s. Think Ingrid Bergman's natural pale-gray tooth enamel sparkling from the screen. But most people don't think of teeth when they recall Ingrid Bergman. The same is true for my mother. Eyes didn't linger on her open smile, warm and engaging though it was. Or her Ingrid-like wide-set eyes and gently angled brows. Or on her soft brown curls or the way her hairline formed a widow's peak in the center of her forehead. Or on the hands that flitted back and forth with a life of their own when she told a story. No, it was her breasts, her enormous breasts, her ninnies, as she called them, to which all eyes gravitated.

In changing rooms at pools where my mother and her big-busted friends took us kids to swim, I watched from behind a towel that covered my undeveloped private parts. I observed their soft full breasts sloped out over bellies with skin stretched and loosened by multiple pregnancies, their nipples well past perky. I watched them stoop and swoop to position their breasts in multiple D-cup bras with sizes somewhere in the forties. I flushed, not they, when they noticed my curious glances as they undressed, toweled off, and dressed again with a complete lack of modesty. Picasso rendered those bodies in paint early in the last century and later in stone.

Once, after a parent meeting at school, my mother and a few other moms regrouped at Elise's house for a glass of wine. Elise had a pool. It was a hot night, and the women decided to take a swim. Of course, no one had a suit. As the story goes,

Elise's husband, who owned the local garbage company, positioned himself at the kitchen sink window that overlooked the pool. There he remained allegedly doing dishes until the skinny-dip ended.

At some point in their uninhibited revelry, the women held a contest, an informal competition of sorts. Lacking the goods to compete, Elise offered to judge. There were three serious contenders for biggest boobs: Lillian, the optometrist's wife; Barbara, whose husband wrote about sports for the local paper, and my mother, married to the vice principal of the high school. To cut to the finish, Mom took first place.

As bits and pieces of this story came to light over the years, I could easily imagine the scene at the pool that night—the nude swim, Elise's husband's impromptu decision to do the dishes, the contest, all retold with much laughter and good-natured quibbling about who really deserved first place.

Mine

The summer I turned 11, I stopped running around bare belly, that is shirtless. Slight swellings had appeared under my nipples, and three coarse dark hairs sprouted between my legs. Finally, I thought. One friend of mine already had her period, and a few girls in my class needed and wore bras.

No sooner had the swelling begun than I wanted a bra—not nearly as much as I wanted a horse, but a lot, and unlike a horse, a bra didn't require my parents' permission or money.

One Saturday, I walked to town with my saved-up allowance—a dollar and a handful of change—stuffed in the pockets of my jeans. I was on a stealth mission like the ones I read about in Nancy Drew mysteries. I ducked into Crislow's Department Store, eased over to underwear, scanned the bras, and snatched one I thought might work. Making sure no one saw me, I took it to a dressing room.

For once when I looked in the full-length mirror, my eyes did not immediately fall on the feature that earned me the nickname Spindle Legs. Instead, all I saw was a size 32-AA white cotton bra with a padded cup, a swatch of white across my ever so slightly expanded chest, a badge of sorts, not exactly earned, but more satisfying than any acquired in Girl Scouts. I tried on my shirt over the bra. No one but me would have noticed the bumps. But that didn't matter. It wasn't the point.

Half floating toward the register, I waited to pay until no one was near, then sneaked the brown paper bag home and hid the bra among my undershirts, to be worn after school and on weekends. It was my little secret, like the tiny buds under it and the hairs between my legs. I still begged my parents for a real horse, and I still rode my stick horse through nearby orchards, but surreptitiously because a voice kept telling me I was too old. Something was different. I didn't know what, just that wearing a bra offered thrills of a new and unfamiliar kind and turned a stick horse silly.

The book my mother gave me about where babies come from used the word "developing" to describe the changes taking place in my body. Thank God for a book and not The Talk. Mom did take me aside one day to show me how a pad and belt worked. "The belts are in the drawer and the Kotex is under the sink. Watch how to attach a pad to the belt," she began. "Just pull the unpadded gauze through like this, and…"

"I get it,"

"I like to tuck—" she continued.

"OK. OK," I said.

"When the time comes—"

"Mom, please."

Ever after, I was on edge when she approached me with a certain smile, as if I was now member of a secret club and she the long-standing member designated to initiate me. I prayed that we would never have another embarrassing exchange, the single such encounter about equipment almost more than I could stand. Everything that was happening to my body was my private business. She must have sensed this because with rare exceptions when she shot me the knowing smile, she left me alone. Then one day out of the blue, she made a foray into forbidden territory.

We were outside at the time. Mom in a rare moment of stillness, wearing a bra and blue pedal pushers, was stretched out on a lounge chair on the lawn, her wet hair wrapped in a towel, her eyes closed. I was reading on the old porch swing—a horse book undoubtedly—with Tippy, my dog and best friend panting nearby in the shade of a jasmine vine that twisted up a redwood pillar to the porch overhang.

"I have an idea," she said, sitting up and smiling her club smile.

Uh, oh, I thought, gripping the book tighter.

"I have to get a new bra," she barreled on, dragging her chair back to the porch. "Why don't you come with me? We'll get one for you too."

I stared down at the page, not saying anything. Shopping! Always an ordeal. Mirrors. Spindle Legs. And for a bra! With Mom. With Mom hovering. No. No way. Besides, I already had one.

"Reading," I managed to spit out.

She pulled the towel off her hair and ran her fingers through it, quick deft strokes.

"Think about it while I get dressed," she said.

She was not taking no for an answer or reading as an excuse. We were in new territory.

A few minutes later, she returned wearing her belted cotton print dress, white with huge orange slices on it. She paused at the swing. I rolled over toward the back.

"I'll do a couple of things first," she said. "Finish the chapter."

I mumbled something about wanting to finish the book.

She dragged a hose through the boxwood hedge. Water sputtered on the raised roots of the iris and splashed on walkway in front of the living room window. I folded down the page I was reading and turned onto my back. From where I lay, her hips and upper arms were visible on either side of a redwood pillar—curves and bulges enhanced by a full skirt with short puffy sleeves all covered in orange slices. It was a style and print made for someone very thin and taller than five-four.

"OK," she called, turning off the water. "Time to get in the car."

And I did. I put the book aside, pulled myself upright, and dragged myself to the driveway. I rode in silence to Crislow's. I nodded when she pointed to one of the bras and sent me to the dressing room with it. But I didn't try it on. I just stood there, heart pounding, face flushed, for a few excruciating minutes. When she asked from a respectful distance how it fit. I said fine, but when she approached the dressing room, I shot my arm out between the curtains, handing her yet another 32 AA.

While she took it and hers to the register, I made a beeline for the door to the street. Mom handed me the Crislow's bag as she settled into the driver's seat. I shoved it to the floor with just a quick glance at the contents. There tucked inside the cup of her double D was my double A, with room for several more.

"What would you like to do now?" Mom asked. "How about we stop at the 5-Spot?"

"Please," I begged. "Just take me home."

"You know, Kathleen," my mother said. "They got in the way when I played tennis."

I think she meant to console me, and if I'd known what would shortly befall her, I might have been nicer. But I was clueless and unsuspecting and a teenager to boot. What could she say helpful or interesting about anything?

Part 2

Life changes in an instant. The ordinary instant.

Joan Didion

Chapter 7
Blindsided: February 19, 1960

I'm slouching in the doorway of the kitchen—age fifteen, five-foot nine, skinny, kinky, reddish-brown hair. Nearby, my short stout mother stoops at the oven. She stabs a baked potato and pokes at a meatloaf. Upright again, still holding the fork, she brushes her permed salt-and-pepper hair off her forehead.

I lift the lid off the pot on one of the back burners—frozen peas. I like the meal my mother's preparing but don't tell her so. I mostly tell her what I don't like. Stew, for example, and barbecued chicken with burned bits on the outside, and my twelve-year-old brother, who is always taking things apart and never putting them back together. "Don't be critical," my father once said to me when I was picking on my brother. Dad rarely corrects me. Mom is the disciplinarian.

"Who'll get the paper?" my father calls from his big chair in the living room. He's watching the news. Queen Elizabeth is in labor with her third child. It'll be a boy, born February 19,1960, the same day our world will fall apart.

Ignoring my father, I watch as my mother slices French bread and tosses a green salad—quick, efficient. "Dinner's almost ready," she says, loud enough for my father to hear. She looks at me and nods at the salad and bread. I roll my eyes, pick up the bowls, and stroll over to the table, keeping my head angled so that I can place them on the yellow Formica without seeing my reflection in the kitchen window. I hate the way I look. Too tall. Too thin.

"Butter too" she says, gesturing toward the counter.

It's margarine, not butter, but I let that go.

Why doesn't *she* get the newspaper, I think and cruise out of the kitchen. Getting the paper's not my job.

"French homework," I shout in the general direction of the living room and head down the hall toward my bedroom.

Through the door to brother's room, I can hear the creak of our ancient card table, and the sound of a screw hitting the floor and rolling. My brother is taking something apart again, maybe another radio. No response from him to my father's request, I note, and consider kicking the door.

At the door to my bedroom, I hesitate, and then stride back toward the living room, my steps echoing off the hardwood floor and bare walls of the hall. From the entryway that overlooks the living room, I see that my father is still in his chair. He looks up.

"I'll go," I tell him, and grab his black, Navy-issue jacket from the hall closet.

The thick padding makes a crinkly sound as I slip my arms as far as they'll go down the long sleeves and wrap the jacket around me like an overcoat. I like the sound it makes as much as the familiar, scratchy feel of its musty, wool lining. I like that it has a history. It kept my father warm while he served on a tanker escort during the Second World War.

Pulling the front door shut behind me, I call for the dog, who's off barking in the neighbor's orchard. The bottom of the hill is not far away but not close either. The porch lights shine on the upper part of the driveway. The lower part is shrouded in darkness, a prune orchard on the downhill side and a row of pepper trees on the other. I am not afraid. Nothing can hurt me. Enveloped in my father's jacket, I am invulnerable.

At dinner, my mother asks the usual question. "How was school?" And I mumble the usual, "Fine." My brother talks about who's coming to his birthday party on Saturday, just two days away. She tells him she'll bake a chocolate cake and then turns back to me.

"What kind of prom dress are you thinking of? Taffeta maybe with a balloon hem? Spaghetti straps are popular."

I hunch down and say nothing. She drones on. Cap sleeves. Satin. Prints. The last thing I want to talk about is a dress for a dance I don't want to go to. The dresses will all look stupid. No one makes clothes for string beans. And who would ask me anyway?

After dinner, my father remains at the table smoking his Chesterfields—white shirt unbuttoned, tie loosened and askew—while my mother clears the dishes and makes coffee in an aluminum percolator. She starts to tell a funny story about a colleague, who is, like her, a high school guidance counselor. Her hands begin their dance, gestures absorbed from old country Italians, and as she signs away, my brother and I slip from the table.

Later, I hear my mother start down the hall to join my father in their room. She stops at my door and knocks. Without waiting for an answer, she opens the door just wide enough to poke her head in. "I'll take you shopping tomorrow after school," she says, "for the formal. We'll try the shopping center." She closes the door without waiting for a response. As her clipped, energetic steps fade, I snap off my lamp and jerk the covers up over my head. There are no dresses for someone like me, not even at the shopping center.

The next morning, my mother drives me to school for orchestra rehearsal as usual. "See you here at four," she says, as she pulls up to the curb. I shrug, grab my violin, and climb out of the car. Without looking back, I walk briskly away.

This is my last memory of ordinary times.

Just before lunch, my father and the principal of my high school, also a family friend, arrive unannounced in my Home Ec class. My father, a principal too, whispers briefly to the startled Mrs. Shrewsberry, who blanches then waves me toward the door. Something is terribly wrong.

Shaking with fear, mouth dry, heart beating fast, I follow my father to a spot down the breezeway where he stops and turns around. His friend walks on out of earshot and waits. "Your mother's been in an accident," my father says. He is facing me when he speaks but not looking at me. Instead, he squints off into the distance, not to a place on campus, but to somewhere deep inside himself. "She's at O'Connor Hospital," he says.

I ask if she'll be OK. He tells me she's unconscious and unable to talk to him yet. "She'll be home in a few days. She'll be fine."

But the content of what he says does not match his strained unfamiliar voice, even less his unheard-of appearance in my classroom. My teeth begin to chatter. When he suggests I might like to leave school for the day, skip the rally for the end-of-the-season basketball game, I know that he is lying. The truth is obvious to me in every clue except his words: My mother has been in an extremely serious accident. She is near death and not expected to live.

On the way to the car, mere yards from where I did not say goodbye that morning, I pause and throw up.

My mother will not meet me at 4 o'clock in front of the high school, as promised. She will not take me on the dreaded shopping trip for a formal. I wonder if she will ever take me anywhere again.

Chapter 8
One Foot Then the Other

Curled as tight as my long legs allowed, I picked at the piping on the satin bedspread. Tears darkened the clusters of pink roses on my pillow. I couldn't stop shivering even in a sweater and jeans. The dog licked my hand and whimpered. Reaching down, I scratched her head and slid onto the thin beige rug next to her. My eyes drifted to the shadow shapes of dead flies inside the glass ceiling fixture, then panned to the dark underside of the dresser and locked on the etched label. Teeth chattering, I snuggled close to Tippy and stared at the blank beige walls of my bedroom then out the window at the leafless almond tree—colorless surroundings that held my attention for little eternities, the basic unit of time in the universe of the unacceptable.

A glimpse of myself in the full-length mirror set the world spinning again. With icy precision and total indifference, the mirror showed someone to whom something catastrophic had happened, not a person who would have her mother back in a few days as promised.

No sound came from Mike's room down the hall. He had faked being sick that morning. Unbeknownst to anyone at the time, he blamed himself for the accident. He had disrupted the morning routine, delayed our mother's departure for work, and this delay placed her in the path of the car that slammed into her from behind.

Throughout the afternoon of February 19, the front door opened and closed as friends and family traipsed in and out. The telephone on the kitchen wall rang a dozen times an hour. I left my room to answer it once while my father was out talking to someone in the driveway.

"Hello, it's Lester Hopping. The carpenter who helped build your house?"

I told him that I remembered him and that my father was not available.

"I just want you all to know how sorry I am about your mother," he said. "She was a great gal."

"Thank you," I managed. But Lester didn't say goodbye. He waited without speaking. Whatever else he expected—comfort, acknowledgment—I didn't have it to give. And why did he say she *was* a great gal?

Toward dinnertime, my mother's parents arrived from San Francisco. Neighbors and friends dropped off casseroles, the first of hundreds of meals.

On the morning following the accident, I was sitting on the porch swing with the dog when two people I didn't know drove up. I guessed they were the owners of the car that struck my mother. I had heard my father say they wanted to stop by. The couple exchanged a few words with Dad at the front door, glanced over at me with stricken expressions, and left.

The days passed. In the vacuum created by my mother's abrupt disappearance, whispered secrets among the grown-ups replaced the loud rise and fall of her voice, the strings of Italian swear words. Conversations now took place in hushed tones behind the closed kitchen doors, the murmur of voices drifting down the hall toward my bedroom. The thick gray layer of loss lay everywhere in the house. Yet certain familiar routines reasserted themselves with variations.

My brother and I returned to school. A classmate's mother volunteered to chauffeur me to early morning orchestra practice. Kind cafeteria ladies at the high school where my father was principal packaged leftovers for him to serve for dinner like the mashed potatoes and brown gravy Mike and I couldn't stand. Dad washed our clothes and made sure we cleaned our rooms. He kept all the balls in the air.

After the accident, I used willpower to keep from falling apart. I called on it throughout the day to *will* my mother back to consciousness and home. And I prayed. Mornings and evenings, I knelt on the thin rug in my room and recited rosaries, begged, pleaded and bargained with God. I made promises, gave ultimatums.

My father drove to the hospital twice a day. "She's not awake yet," he told us time and time again. "She had a cerebral hemorrhage," he explained.

Sometimes my brother and I accompanied Dad on his evening visits. I always changed into a good dress and heels—church clothes—maybe to please Mom, should I be allowed to see her, but more likely so I'd feel grown-up and in control.

Mike and I sat silently in the lobby near the white marble statue of the blessed Virgin Mary and waited for our father to summon us to our mother's room. Now and then, a nursing nun would pass by. When I couldn't sit any longer, I paced. Click-tap click-tap, my footfalls echoed off the marble floor of the hospital lobby, in cheerless counterpoint to how powerless I felt.

"She's not awake yet," our father repeated, each time he rejoined us.

We didn't see our mother until shortly before her discharge three months later. I didn't know what to expect when the night of our first visit finally arrived. Dad had told us that when she first woke, she asked if they'd had a baby boy or a baby girl. I thought this was funny. My mother used to be funny. Was she still going to be? Would she be herself at all?

When Mike and I entered the room, she was lying flat on her back in her hospital gown. The top sheet hung so that her left leg was exposed. She had a way of moving as unique as a fingerprint—quick, deliberate, precise—and when she lifted her leg a few inches off the sheet and set it down again, I recognized her style instantly. Relief flowed through me. She was still funny, and one other thing hadn't changed, even if it was only the way she moved her leg.

"Say hi to your mother," Dad said, motioning us to approach the bed.

She looked so different—forty pounds lighter, her face un-lined, her hair long and straight and brushed back. She smelled different too. A bottle of pink Desert Flower lotion sat on her bedside table. The room reeked of it. I came to hate that smell.

"Say hello," our father prompted. Mom looked at us blank-ly for a few seconds, turned her head away, and began to sob.

Dad took her hand. She pulled away and rolled onto her side. "She'll be OK," he said, and motioned for us to leave.

As best I could, I tamped down seething feelings of terror and had another chat with God.

In mid-May, an ambulance delivered Mom home. My grand-mother watched from driveway, my father beside her, and me not far away. As the attendants unloaded the gurney, Dad leaned down and whispered to Nanny what one of the hospital nurses had said to him when Mom was discharged. "This is just the beginning."

Beginning! Surely not. My mother's return home was sup-posed to mark the *end* of the terrible times. Didn't her return mean that soon we would have our lives back? Wouldn't it be only a matter of time before we'd get *her* back, *all* of her? Wouldn't rehab fix her? Teach her to walk again, to speak? And if not, wouldn't our love and prayers bring her back?

My mother resumed her place at the center of our family, but now it was her needs that held her there, not her high spir-its and energy. She was different, damaged, more like a little kid. Mornings, she resisted getting up. Our ignorant family doctor prescribed Dexedrine, a wake-up pill, and to counteract it, a sleeping pill. Month in and month out, my mother spent her days in her room—the double bed next to her hospital bed a constant reminder of the life she lost.

I couldn't understand why she chose to isolate herself. I longed for her to want to be a part of our lives again, to make us laugh. Why didn't she beg her nurse to help her with walking and strengthening unused muscles? The mother I had known was not a quitter.

To the familiar sounds around our house—the squeaky door of the Norge refrigerator, the squish of the weather-stripping meeting the sill of the front door, the dog barking in the or-chard—new sounds were added. At night after homework, Mike and I joined Dad to watch TV in the living room. Mom rang the cowbell to signal she needed something. Bedpan? Wa-ter? Company? My father left us. Sometimes, he didn't come back before our bedtime. On our way to our rooms, we heard the drone of Dad's calm voice and Mom's sobs and screams.

"I wan' to die. Le' me die."

My mouth went dry. I felt like throwing up.

I wondered what Dad was saying to comfort her. That she'd get better? That he loved her? Please, Dorothy, the kids. But no words could soothe her. She had lost everything.

Just don't let her die, I reminded God.

The radio in my bedroom didn't drown out the screams, clangs, and bangs when Mom hit the rail of her bed or the win-dows beside it, just short of shattering them. I tried pulling up the covers and putting a pillow over my head. When that was still not enough to silence the sounds of her misery, I dragged my radio under the covers, the acrid scent of warm plastic somehow comforting.

Please stop screaming. Please stop crying. *Please don't die.*

After a while, I felt the vibration of my father's heavy footsteps on his way to the phone. Twenty minutes later, there'd be a knock at the front door, then footsteps again and deep voices in the hall. My mother's screams would sound louder for a moment as the bedroom door opened and shut again. Seconds later, she'd fall silent.

At breakfast the next morning, no one mentioned what happened in the middle of the night. Were my father's lips pressed together a little more tightly? Were the lines that radiated from the outside corners of his eyes deeper? Was he wincing because his ulcer was acting up?

My brother and I picked at our eggs and toast. The nurse arrived. Mom started crying again. No, no, she won't get up. Our father left for work. My brother and I left for school. We all carried on. What else was there to do? First one day, then another, we lived our lives.

In my negotiations with the Almighty, I granted a generous extension and settled in to wait out the ten years it would take for our lives to reverse their trajectory again, one small eternity after another.

Chapter 9
Can't Stop the World

At school, I pretended nothing had changed. I saw friends and attended club meetings. I did homework, took tests, and wrote papers. If I could avoid speaking in class, I did. Only my world history teacher called on me when I didn't have my hand up, his way of forcing me to re-engage.

Apart from one classmate named Peggy, no one at school asked about my mother. Peggy sought me out every day in the months following the accident. She had recently moved to the US from Australia and knew me from Home Ec class where my father appeared the morning of Mom's accident. I'd stiffen and look away when I spotted her coming at me. Tall, blond, athletic, she'd walk right up anyway and plant herself in my face, taking no clues from my evasive maneuvers. "How's your mum?" she'd ask in her soft lilting accent. Then she'd squint, cock her head, and wait.

"The same," I'd say, staring at the ground, heart pounding, legs trembling, my defenses breached.

Her daily check-in complete, Peggy would depart. And that was that until the next day. Just that. For months.

Meanwhile, I tried to blend in. Costumes for the spring play? Sure, I'll help. Collect money for orphans in Peru? OK.

But with a sixteen-year-old's ramped up anxiety, insecurity, and dread compounded by an unfathomable loss, every time a messenger entered my classroom with a pink summons slip, I assumed it was for me and that my mother was dead. With no one to talk to who'd lost a parent to death or illness, I barely stayed afloat.

In the vacuum of my mother's absence, roles and responsibilities at home shifted. After the accident, I was still her daughter, but she was not my mother—not the mother she used to be. I did for her. She did not do for me. I took care of her when my father had to go to evening meetings. She couldn't be left alone. Who was the parent? Who was the child?

Dad took over the grocery shopping and most of the cooking. Once known for his scrambled eggs at Sunday breakfast, he branched out to fried chicken and gravy but placed the raw chicken pieces into cold oil and mixed the flour and broth to gravy consistency before heating them. His signature dish was what he called green salad—pears stuffed with cream cheese in lime jello.

To supplement his cooking, cafeteria workers from the high school still sent leftover food, and the Faculty Wives delivered weekly dinners. But the best meals, not that I appreciated them, came from Aunt Mary, Uncle Vincent's wife and a professional cook. Mom had always told us her salads were the best. Her spaghetti sauce and egg custard too. That was saying something in a family with four chefs.

One day as I was leaving my best friend's house, her mother handed me a recipe. "Use an electric frying pan," she said. "It's a quick dinner—pork chops, sliced onions, and Campbell's mushroom soup." She didn't ask how things were at home. She didn't take me aside and listen or offer advice. With six children to look after, all she could offer was a recipe. I made the dish a few times but otherwise left the cooking to my father, the washing up afterward too.

He never asked me to do more. He never complained either or expressed resentment about his added responsibilities, or about anything really. He went about doing what needed to be done, giving Mike and me the space to have the most normal life possible under the circumstances.

Like our mother, he expected us to feed the dog and cat and to clean our rooms even though he kept the housekeeper Mom had hired when she returned to full-time work. But unlike her, he initiated a white glove inspection of our rooms on Saturday mornings.

We met him in the hallway, followed him into my room, and stood silently by as he ran his finger across the top of my dresser and along the windowsill. He looked up to check the corners for cobwebs and lifted the bedspread to peer underneath. Same in Mike's room. If we passed—and we always did—Dad gave us each a dime.

Often on Saturdays, Uncle Vincent worked at the house—mowing, pruning, and planting. I could hear his grunts and asthmatic wheeze from indoors, but it never occurred to me to take on any chores beyond my room.

Nanny spent weekends at our house, caring for Mom so Dad could have a break and play golf. I felt sorry for her, not because she worked catering jobs all week and cleaned and cooked and ironed at her house and ours—I had little appreciation for such things as a teenager. What hurt my heart was the way Mom ignored her. My chest tightened every time Nanny approached my mother. "Dorothy, are you OK?" she'd ask, her face taut with concern.

If at all, Mom responded with a shrug.

"Dorothy, how about a sangwich?"

Mom's eyes flashed. She'd never allowed Mike and me to use the Italian pronunciation.

"Or a cup of coffee?"

Mom kept her eyes down or just stared out the window. In these unbearably awkward moments, Nanny's arms dropped to her sides. Her body sagged. If she was holding a dust cloth or dishrag, she passed it from one hand to the other, blinking rapidly, her lips pressed together. "I'll be back in a while," she'd say.

Disinhibited by her brain injury, Mom gave silent hurtful expression to her grievances from childhood.

I loved Nanny and she loved me. I didn't try to understand what had gone on between my mother and her long ago. I knew only what Nanny had confided one Easter vacation when she invited me back to San Francisco to spend a few days alone with her. On the first day of my visit, we took the bus downtown and had lunch at Blum's. Her hair was blue that day. She had aimed for grey but applied too much of what was in the bottle under the bathroom sink.

The next day, she worked. In her sixties and still a sought-after professional cook, she catered big events in hotels and smaller ones in the homes of the social elite of San Francisco. When she returned home, she changed out of her black uniform and into a house dress and a cotton print apron, ironed, the ties secured in a neat bow. Hugging her was like hugging a tree trunk. She never removed her full-body corset until bedtime.

"Would you like a sangwich?" she said.

I turned down the sandwich and followed her into the kitchen, a room barely big enough for a small table, a tiny ice box—as she called it—and a gas range. She filled the kettle, humming tunelessly under her breath.

"This range is a good one," she said, switching on a burner. "but I have ideas for how to make it better."

I couldn't imagine redesigning a stove. I was planning to teach one day, a fine profession in her mind and possibly equally unimaginable to her. Lighting one of her unfiltered cigarettes, she mentioned how much she regretted not having an education. I told her she'd done very well without one. She commented on how slim I was and asked how I stayed that way. I said I paid attention but not much. She set our cups on the table, and we pulled out two stools. She had never told me much about her past, so I was surprised when she began to describe an event that occurred over forty years earlier, a story with clues to what shaped her life and in turn, my mother's, and mine.

When she was thirteen, she left home to clean and cook for wealthy families in San Francisco. She sent a portion of her wages home to Gram. By age seventeen, the year her father died, she had a husband and daughter, Dorothy, my mother. But there were problems.

One Tuesday—not Sunday, her usual visiting day—she took the train to Los Gatos. Instead of looking out the window, she fidgeted in her seat. Her mother had reared three children on her own and traveled with them across an ocean and a continent to rejoin her husband and two older sons. What's more, her mother was a devout Catholic and believed her reward would come in the next life. It was unlikely she would consent to the request that had brought my grandmother to Los Gatos that day.

Willing to risk the eternal damnation of her soul but unwilling to act without her mother's approval, my grandmother trudged up College Avenue rehearsing her appeal. She found her mother weeding in the vegetable garden. They sat together in leather barrel chairs on the porch speaking Piemontese, a dialect from the north of Italy, and the only language her mother ever knew.

My grandmother described her husband's absences, his drinking, his refusal to work and support their baby. "And I can't take Dorothy to my job anymore," she said. "Mrs. Spreckels told me to put her up for adoption, that she would have a better life with a family who could care for her."

Her mother's response was swift and unexpected. "Bring Dorothy to live with me. And as to your marriage, you must do what makes you happy."

And so it was settled. At age nineteen, my grandmother divorced her husband and sent my two-year-old mother to live with her mother on College Avenue.

When Nanny came to the end of her story that day in her kitchen, the furrows between her brows softened. For a few seconds, she held her breath, her eyes unfocused as she looked inward and back. Then her shoulders dropped, and she exhaled, looking at me with same mix of disbelief and relief and profound gratitude she surely felt on that long-ago Tuesday. But her decision had consequences.

Maybe my mother could have forgiven her for sending her away when she was two, but I knew that when remarriage brought stability and another child to my grandmother's life, she hadn't taken my mother back to live with her. Along with everything else that had changed after the accident, my mother stopped speaking to her mother altogether.

Repeatedly rebuffed on the weekends she spent at our house after the accident, my grandmother never said a word. She continued to come, fifty-two times a year for most of a decade.

With my mother missing, substitutes trickled into the space she left behind. A friend of hers from nursery school took me to the Mother-Daughter Breakfast at our church, an event where I might have felt out of place without a stand-in. I appreciated the kind gesture but felt uncomfortable nevertheless. The stockbroker's wife, who never again visited Mom—she couldn't bear to see her *that way*—invited me to their family cabin at Lake Tahoe and bought me a prom dress, a print one with spaghetti straps like the one my mother mentioned the night before her accident. Again, a kind gesture.

And then one day on my way home from the school bus stop, I fell into step with a young mother pushing a stroller. Short and trim with fashionably frosted hair, she introduced herself. "Judie DeKlotz."

I felt obliged to tell her my name and that I was a junior at Saratoga High School. "My father's the principal at Los Gatos High," I added. Nothing more.

But she continued. "We just moved into the adobe up the street. You must know the one. The bricks were made on the property." Unfamiliar with the house and its history, I peeked into the stroller. Babies interested me more than houses. "Her name is Andrea," Judie said.

From under a cap, the baby's light brown hair fell across her forehead, her blue eyes open wide. "Aw, she's cute," I said.

"She's nine months old," Judie said. "And she's blind. I was exposed to German measles when I was pregnant." Her tone was matter-of-fact.

I didn't know what to say. I tried to imagine how she must have felt when she was told that her child would never see. I wondered if "exposed" hinted that she blamed the person who gave her the measles. How did she feel about that person?

I agonized over the stranger who hit my mother's car. Uninsured and unlicensed, he demolished our lives. Because this happened when I was the most disconnected from my mother, he also took away our opportunity to apologize, to make peace, to heal our relationship. But blame didn't change a thing. It only made for more misery.

All in all, I wondered less about Judie's experience than Andrea's. What would it be like to live without sight? Curious but trying not to stare, I gazed down at the baby again. She appeared perfectly normal. "Hi, Andrea," I said, and touched her hand with my finger. She grabbed on. Something in me softened.

By the time Judie said goodbye at my driveway, I had learned about her growing up years in Southern California and that she was married to Fred, a lawyer, whom she met when they were students at Berkeley. Five minutes later, she knocked on my front door. "By any chance, do you babysit?" she asked.

"I have," I told her, pleased to be asked by this stranger, "just not lately."

Judie said nothing as if waiting for me to continue.

"My mother was in a car accident nine months ago," I blurted.

A look of concern settled on her face. "I'm so sorry. How is she?"

"She has a nurse now," I said.

I don't remember whether Judie said more or I just sensed she understood the enormity of my loss. The moment passed. She smiled. "About babysitting, I'd like to hire you."

I had the feeling she would stand there at my front door until I agreed.

Soon, I was spending most Saturday nights cuddling with Andrea and talking to her as if she were mine. Judie encouraged me to hang out at her house whenever I wanted, and I did. I was flattered. Warm, friendly, and talkative, she seemed interested in me as a person—in which subjects I liked, the books I read, and my friends and future plans. In turn, she had someone to entertain Andrea.

I never thought about the overlap in our situations—that Judie had a blind daughter, and I had a disabled mother, that both our lives had changed in unexpected ways. Just as I paid little attention to her daughter's blindness, Judie overlooked my mother's paralysis and garbled speech. She visited my parents at our house and chatted with my father about school affairs. She greeted my mother by name and found things to talk about with her. When my mother was able, Judie invited our whole family to dinner. Only one of my parents' friends ever did that.

Cosmopolitan in tastes and interests and a gourmet cook, Judie introduced me—a picky eater—to what she called Persian-style rice (with a raw egg, plain yogurt, and chopped onion), and to a Kosher deli, Caesar salad, and beet aspic, which I was too shy to turn down. She took me to the ballet in San Francisco and to lunch in a big hotel before the performance. Later, when I was about to leave for college, she took me shopping at her friend's preppy clothing store.

"Are you familiar with Villager?" she asked, showing me the label on a dress. "Or Ladybug?"

I shook my head.

"Or Geist & Geist sweaters? They're classic."

These words turned out to be code for very expensive clothes. Except for a single Lantz dress my mother bought for me when I was thirteen, I'd never seen prices like the ones on the garments Judie pulled from the shelves.

She insisted on buying me two G&G sweaters—one green, the other beige—and a Villager wool jumper I eventually wore out.

"Let's get the orange bathrobe with the grey polka dots too," she said. "You can wear it in the dorm and next year in the sorority." I cringed. The bathrobe might grow on me but never the idea of a sorority. It had come up a few times, but I had no interest in becoming a Tri Delt as she had.

"I'm having lunch later this week with a sorority sister," she continued.

"Uh huh," I said, bracing myself for another of her pitches.

"Tri Delt is a good house, and Berkeley's a big place," she continued.

"Uh huh," I said.

"I'll help you get in. You'll have ready-made friends."

"Hm," I said, horrified at the notion.

"I met Fred at a mixer."

"Oh."

"Well?"

"Maybe," I said, too shy to express my feelings. I was just not a sorority girl, and I knew it. A classic sweater? OK. But dress and behavior codes? Rules and restrictions? Not for me. Besides, I was not a part of the social swirl in high school, and those were the girls who joined. A sorority? Over my dead body I thought, and politely held my ground. I'd make my own friends.

One afternoon, she led me into her bathroom, took a cotton ball and dabbed an exfoliant on my face. "There," she said.

"Stick with Bonne Belle products. They're the best at controlling pimples."

Embarrassed but appreciative, I took her suggestions about skin care and about how to wear my hair too. She sent me to her stylist, who gave me a "cap cut," a short practical hairdo.

We also shared a love of horses. Judie indulged my fantasies about owning one. "My father bought me my first horse when I was three," she told me.

"My father brought me a gigantic blue painted one from a barn dance he chaperoned. He taped it to my bedroom wall while I was asleep. 'Don't say I never gave you a horse,' he told me in the morning."

"The neighbors have an empty corral," Judie said. "Let's ask if they'd mind if we kept a horse there."

This would never have occurred to me, and I was excited. But it turned out the neighbors did mind. Too many flies. Dream dashed again just as years earlier when I had brought up a horse with my mother. She'd laughed and said, "Don't be ridiculous. No money to buy it. No place to keep it."

I don't know what my father thought about how close I'd become to Judie and her family. As far as I knew, in my mother's mind, taking care of Judie's daughter was time well spent. Mom had been a teacher after all. She loved children as did I. And I was earning money. In the year after the accident, Mike too spent less and less time at home, and once he had a driver's license, he kind of disappeared. With his mother disabled in an accident Mike believed he had caused and a father consumed by work and caregiving, my brother found another family, an intact one with two healthy parents and four lively blond daughters. They welcomed him, fed him, and asked his opinions.

During that first year without the mother we had known, we kept coming up against the things she had always done. Who would make the first Thanksgiving dinner she couldn't, send Christmas cards, and hang holiday decorations? Judie dictated simple instructions over the phone, and I cooked my first Thanksgiving turkey. I don't remember if Mom got out of bed that day, but if so, she had returned by the time of my grandmother's unexpected visit—Nanny thrown off too by the abrupt end of our traditional gatherings back when my mother was mobile and cordial. Picking at a bit of turkey skin, my grandmother complimented my efforts. "You'll want to remove the stuffing before carving," she said and fetched a spoon. "And the innards before cooking," she said smiling and holding up the paper-wrapped parcel she'd retrieved from inside the cooked bird. Embarrassed, I said I couldn't find it when I felt around, so I thought maybe this turkey was missing its inner parts.

As to decorating the house for Christmas, the Faculty Wives—or maybe Flying Needle, my mother's sewing group formed during WWII—came to the rescue. They decked the living room with a forest of greens that filled the house with their scent.

One afternoon toward Christmas Day, Dad discovered me at a card table in the living room sending cards to the hundred people who had sent them to us. "Not necessary," he said.

"Mom would have."

"You don't have to do that."

"She can't so I am,"

"It's not important."

But to me, it was. How about continuity? In our new reality, filling in for my mother was part of a holding pattern, an attempt to maintain a fragile equilibrium until she returned.

Chapter 10
Glimmers

Deep in my negotiations with God, I was going for a miracle. Not of the Lourdes sort. Not the tossing aside crutches kind. I expected my mother would have to work at getting back to normal. But hadn't she thrived after growing up poor and abandoned? She lived through the Depression and two world wars, and a husband who left to fight in one during the first years of their marriage. At my Mom's core was a "move on" and "next step" person.

Instead of behaving according to my expectations and hopes, she refused to engage in her recovery. Where was the mother I planned to reconnect with after years of my bad behavior? This new mother resisted therapy—cognitive, speech, physical, and occupational. Her loud protests carried to my room. Didn't she want to get better? "Get up out of that bed, and get going," I wanted to shout. "Right now." But deeply disappointed, I stood by uncomprehending and frustrated and angry as the distance between us grew. I blamed her for not working hard enough.

Talk therapy might have benefited the family—if not my stubborn mother then the rest of us. But at the time, only the diagnosed mentally ill saw psychiatrists or psychologists. People didn't delve into their feelings or openly share them, and one-way chats with God to share how I felt were just that, one way. And perhaps more than most, our family stiff-upper-lipped it and carried on. "Suffer in silence" was my father's mantra throughout my childhood when we complained about cuts, bruises, blisters, mosquito bites, or sunburns. Like Mom, my brother, father, and I each grappled with our changed lives on our own.

A year after the accident, my mother's doctors concluded she had reached "maximum medical improvement." She wouldn't get any better. My father petitioned to become her guardian so that she would be eligible for retirement benefits at age forty-five. At the hearing, the Superior Court of California declared her an "incompetent person," and she lost the legal right to manage her own life. But my father didn't tell me any of this. And I wouldn't have accepted it anyway. I had another outcome in mind and remained ever on the alert for positive change

Sure enough, despite my mother's dismal prognosis, flickers of her old self began to reappear, scarcely noticeable at first—in the way an intermittent hum from somewhere in the house, easy to dismiss at first, all at once becomes unmistakable.

Mom's friend Jane, a devout Catholic and the same woman who took me to the mother-daughter breakfast at church, came to the house one day to visit. Tall, thin, beautiful, and rich, she took a seat on the edge of one of the maple chairs in our living room. "Dorothy," she said, after she filled my mother in on what her boys were up to, "a friend of mine would like to visit you."

My mother didn't say anything.

"I think you'll like him. He's a priest," Jane continued. "Would it be OK?"

Was Jane's motive salvation? I'll never know, but with a nod—Mom would never say no to Jane—she agreed to a visit from a stooped, grey-haired, and exceedingly kind Jesuit priest named Father Healy. Not particularly religious, my mother had never befriended a priest. But on the following Wednesday afternoon, with her nurse holding her up, my mother made her way from her bedroom to the living room, one halting step at a time, the heavy brace on her right leg clanking, her panicky yelps echoing down the hallway. Drawn to the unusual visit of a priest to our house, I sat in on it. The mere presence of someone with a direct line to the Almighty had to be a good thing.

Father Healy pulled up a chair opposite the couch where Mom sat. He opened the Baltimore Catechism, a guide I remembered as a six-year-old making my first communion. "Who made you?" he asked.

Childish though the question was, Mom squinted and looked up at the ceiling, searching for the answer. "I don' know. Who...ma'...me?"

"God made you, Dorothy," Father Healy told her, and continued to the second question.

"Why did God make you?"

Mom's forehead wrinkled as she thought. "Why?" she said, after a pause.

Father Healy got as far as, "God made you in his image to…," when Mom interrupted.

"Fa'er," she said, lifting her good arm to give emphasis to the words that followed, a semblance of the gestures that had once accompanied everything she said. "Do you know how they ma' ho-y wa-er?" And without pausing, she went on, speeding up and laughing as she approached the punch line. "They pu" it on the sto' and boi' the hell ou' of it!"

"Mom," I said, embarrassed that she had sworn in front of a priest, even in the telling of a joke, yet secretly pleased too.

To his credit, Father Healy smiled before continuing with the lesson.

Just before he left, he asked my mother to read a few pages ahead in the catechism, but the blue and white booklet remained untouched on the windowsill near her bed next to a bottle of Holy Water from Lourdes, also untouched.

The visits lasted for years, never varying. Week in and week out, Father Healy gracefully resigned himself to posing the same questions in the catechism and smiling at the joke Mom relished telling him at every visit. He always listened as if for the first time. For her, it always was.

I don't know what this priest thought of those visits. Surely, he intended to minister to her spiritual needs, not be her straight man. But the joy of her laughter must have touched him. It did me, and I was grateful for it and for him.

Besides perking up for visits from Father Healy, Mom started to play Solitaire. Just as she remembered some things from before the accident, she remembered a few games. Soon Uncle Vincent delivered a tray-size piece of plywood he covered in green felt so Mom could play in bed. At the same time, he also scolded her for spending too much time there, and she took to calling him "brunsung," the word for growly bear in their Italian dialect. Using her new table, she laid out the cards in messy piles with her good hand and played by her adapted rules. They should have given her an edge, but she hardly ever won and didn't seem to care.

Around the time the Solitaire games started up, Mom's fun-loving nature made an appearance one night when Mike and I were staying with her. Dad was at a meeting. Instead of watching TV, we joined her in her bedroom. She told us to crank her bed to sitting. On impulse, I fetched a veiled black felt hat from her closet and put it on her. She turned her head one way and the other as if to show it off. Next Mike got a necklace and bracelet out of her jewelry box, and I rummaged in her purse for her compact and powdered her nose. Then I took out her bright red lipstick. She opened her mouth, making an effort to stretch her lips taut while I applied the lipstick, some of which made it to her lips. Next, Mike and I dressed her in a navy-blue silk blouse.

"Surprise!" we cried when my father opened the bedroom door. His expression ran the gamut from shock to curiosity and amusement, and finally to something I couldn't place, but sad comes close. For a second, I worried that Mike and I might have gone too far with our dress-up game—Mom did look kind of silly—but her obvious glee removed the doubt.

Over the first few years, my mother progressed from remaining in bed to making her way to the living room one or two days a week, then three out of five, and then most weekdays.

"Dorothy, stay up and watch my soap with me," Mom's new nurse suggested one day.

Soon, the new weekday routine included *The Edge of Night* at 3:30, and Mom stopped begging to go to bed after lunch.

"Dorothy, how about watching *I Love Lucy*," my father asked one night.

Not only did she stay up for it but for other evening TV shows too like *Bonanza* and *Perry Mason*, shows with characters that she had once enjoyed. And she appeared to follow the plots, but I never knew for sure.

"Your mother walked between bars today at PT," my father told Mike and me at dinner one night, clearly pleased. "With help," he added.

She also began "practicing walking" on weekdays with her nurse. Up and down the hall they went, the thuds of Mom's orthopedic shoes and clank of her brace marking her uneven gait. But with atrophied muscles and no sense of balance, she made no measurable progress relearning this instinctive skill. "Ho' me, ho' me, ho' me," she cried, terrified of falling. Meanwhile, every time she needed to get to the bathroom or kitchen or car, someone had to hold her up while she took one unsteady step at a time. I never minded being the one. To me, this was evidence that her old self hadn't vanished entirely and that the blaze of whatever had overcome challenges still smoldered.

But when she said one day, "When I wake up, I thin' I ca' wa'k'," I began to wonder if she realized that being unable to walk was the least of her problems. If she woke up and could walk, what then? Did she forget that she couldn't remember? But she seemed oblivious to cognitive changes. As for me, dwelling on her losses only brought on bouts of feeling sorry for myself. It was all so unfair. Why her? Why us? And why wouldn't God fix it all?

Chapter 11
Silence

For eight years, uniformed nurses cared for my mother during the day. She hated all but the first, a tough young Irish woman named Isabella Watts, who threatened to stand Mom on her head if she didn't get out of bed—and on several occasions, did just that. Mom loved her.

When Mrs. Watts gave notice shortly before I left for college in 1962, I wondered how our family would survive. What would we do without her good-humored, no-nonsense approach to my mother? God was silent on this subject as He'd been on all others. My father must have tried to persuade Mrs. Watts to stay, but she had made up her mind to leave. I never knew the reason but could guess. The challenges of working with my mother wore her out.

After Mrs. Watts left, Mom stayed in bed. She ignored the new nurse, who left in short order, and screamed at the third, who quit as well. I was away at Berkeley when Dad placed Mom in a rest home.

I didn't ask for an explanation, and he didn't give one, the reasons obvious. Her stay there would last nine months, and although her memory was spotty at best after her accident, she never forgot it. "Jus' pu' me in a home," she'd say, whenever Dad expressed the tiniest frustration.

Throughout my freshman year, I took the bus home to Los Gatos on the weekends, but one particular weekend in the winter of 1963, my father telephoned and offered to pick me up. It never occurred to me to ask why. When he pulled up in front of my dorm, I slid onto the white leather seat of his car. He had come directly from work and was wearing a favorite tweed sport coat and a pale green and grey striped necktie, the ever-present cigarette tucked between the first two fingers of his right hand. What I remember most about that ride is silence.

We began the drive home in our separate worlds, with our own thoughts, yet content to be together. As he turned onto the freeway, I asked how Mom was doing.

"About the same," he said, his face relaxed except for the crows feet that mimicked those of men who gaze across great distances. His came from looking inward.

"She's made friends with an Italian man. They eat together in the dining room," he told me, grateful she was adapting to her new situation. "You know your mother," he added, referring to my mother's ability to befriend strangers, a gift compromised but not destroyed by her accident.

I said nothing, overcome with guilt for how much I'd resented being held hostage to her outgoing ways when I was little, how at the gas station and market, in the line at the bank, wherever she found herself, she chatted with friends, acquaintances, and even total strangers, while my brother and I stood on one leg then the other until she finished.

Dad interrupted my thoughts. "Dorothy Baird said your mother had the best personality of anyone she had ever met." Mrs. Baird was a friend and had been one of Mom's high school teachers. My father repeated the friend's remark in a musing sort of way, speaking aloud, but almost more to himself than to me.

"If your mother had just bent over to tie her shoe that morning," he said, in the same abstracted tone, this remark the second of the only two references ever to *his* experience of my mother's accident, oblique both of them. Mom was wearing high heels on the day of the accident. It was a metaphorical "if only" emerging from his memory of the person my mother had been before the loss of much that defined her.

My father's words hung in the air for a moment, then dissipated like the smoke from his cigarette.

I wanted to let him know I recognized his suffering but was at a loss for what to say, and his pain frightened me. A part of me wished he wouldn't express his feelings aloud at all, even obliquely, even if half to himself. I was still engaged in a moment-to-moment struggle to fake a normal life and pass for someone on whom the sky had not fallen.

Neither of us said anything for a few minutes.

Breaking the silence, my father asked how my classes were going.

"Fine," I said, and left it at that. The far-away look settled on his face again. He seemed too preoccupied to listen to a story about how my French teacher had held the class spellbound when she acted out scenes from Racine's *Phedre*. I let the urge pass to tell him about this astonishing performance and settled for believing that he was happy for me and didn't need any details. I also renewed my pledge to keep to myself anything that might cause him to worry, like the fact that I had been served a Pink Lady at a bar.

Thus, variations of silence mingled in an awkward dance between us, as much a way of communicating as speaking. The comfortable silence of two quiet, private people who love each other. The selective silence of any nineteen-year-old with a parent. And finally, a silence that was an on-going reaction to loss. Also in the mix was the reason for Dad's offer of a ride home.

We entered the house together and stepped into a strange silence. "Where's Tippy?" I asked, scanning the living room from the entry hall. The dog usually greeted me in the driveway. My father didn't say anything. The lines around his eyes deepened. He glanced at me and then looked away again. "Where is she?" I repeated, anxious. The small, ordinary mutt from the pound, my best friend, had seen me through the ordinary and extraordinary changes that had taken place between the ages of nine and nineteen. She licked a decade's worth of tears. She stayed by my side the day of my mother's accident when all our lives changed. She provided the comfort no human could during the years that followed.

"Tippy's dead," he said softly, shoving his hands deep into his pockets.

I stepped toward him as if I hadn't heard the words he had spoken with such difficulty.

"What?" I said, incredulous that he hadn't mentioned this as soon as he'd picked me up. "How?"

"Chasing a car," he told me. I expected him to go on, but the only sound was the muted clink of coins from his pocket.

"Why didn't you tell me? I don't understand why you didn't tell me right away." Stunned by my father's inexplicable decision to withhold the news, and in shock from the loss, I blamed him for the dog's death. Tippy wouldn't have died if I'd been taking care of her. I ran out the door into the nearby orchard and later to Judie's. She knew how hard it was to lose a pet and offered me her car if I thought a drive might help.

My father's delay in telling me about Tippy lodged in my memory. I would occasionally stumble over it, a puzzling incident—truly not a big deal—but impossible to remove or bury or fully understand until decades later.

Early one morning when my own daughters were already grown and gone, our family dog Tessa died. She had seen both girls through their teens and early twenties. Should I call the girls before they left for work, interrupt their breakfasts with bad news? Maybe not. Why spoil the day? And really, a few hours wouldn't matter.

On the other hand, maybe they would want to know right away. I decided to delay letting them know until that night. The instant I postponed delivering the bad news, I found myself transported back to 1963, to the front seat of my father's car, riding home on that winter weekend, only this time I was in the driver's seat.

My father *had* intended to tell me about the dog soon after he picked me up. Instead, he gave me one more hour free from the pain of loss, a gift he had been unable to give me when my mother lay in a coma after her accident.

Silence is complex. It can be insufficient, insensitive, and cruel. It can also be caring and kind, and even proof of love. In my life, it has been all of these things, sometimes simultaneously.

Chapter 12
Against the Odds

The biggest change I encountered on one of my visits home came galloping at me the minute I walked through the front door. Barking loudly, the German Shepherd lunged at my throat, teeth bared. My father grabbed her by the collar and held her while I squeezed by and joined my mother in the living room. "He' na' is Kim," Mom said excitedly. "K for Kath'een, an' M for Mi…chael." Mom had grown up around generations of Uncle Vincent's shepherds and loved the breed, but she was even more thrilled that the dog had come already named for her children.

My father explained that Kim had spent the first two years of her life cooped up indoors while her owner, an older woman who lived alone, was at work.

"We took her as a favor," he said. "She bonded instantly with your mother. Isn't she beautiful?"

This coming from someone who was not a dog person. Kim growled at me. Winning her over would take some time, but there was no doubt she was here to stay. If taking Kim had been a favor, it also turned out to be a blessing, only not right away.

To my mother's delight, Kim didn't allow just anyone in the room with her. Charging across the living room with threatening growls, the dog warned off almost everyone who approached, and actually anyone Mom didn't care to have near her—like her own mother. Except for my father, the dog rejected men and had to be restrained in their presence. Over Kim's lifetime, she bit every one of my mother's friends when they forgot and turned their backs to her. But no one complained. They recognized that the dog helped my mother in ways doctors, friends, and even loved ones could not—Mom and Kim's mutual needs for unconditional love, acceptance, and companionship made a perfect match.

"Di' you fee' Kim?" and "Does the dog… ha' water?" my mother asked dozens of times a day.

She couldn't make a meal or even a sandwich, but the dog's needs placed her back in supervisory caregiver mode, restoring purpose to her life, even if others did the actual chores.

Kim came to love my father and accept me and my brother, whose introduction to the new member of our family took place when he returned on leave from the South China Sea. Mike had never liked school, and aware he would be drafted if he didn't go straight to college, he joined the Navy after high school—without consulting anyone. "At least he's safer on water," my father said, his brow pinched.

"No whee'cha', no whee'cha'," my mother insisted four years out, determined to walk again on her own. She agreed to use a walker, however, another big change. I guess the walker filled a need without telegraphing a message of permanence the way a wheelchair did. Her walker had armrests and a bench inside a metal frame on wheels, so she could sit securely and use her good leg to push. Though stairs prevented her from entering our living room and she still required help in the bathroom, her limited mobility had the flavor of a miracle, if not the one I'd ordered. Checking in one weekend, I noted signs of her new-found independence—gouges on cupboards and door jambs and along the pale green walls of the hallway.

Yet another significant change occurred when Mom's best friend Barbara arranged a weekly bridge game that quickly became the high point of Mom's week. Barbara, Billie, and Marion—The Friends, as the card players come to be known— showed up every Tuesday at noon with their sandwiches. They didn't expect to play serious, fast-paced bridge. They didn't care about taking home the pot, important though the money was to my mother. Instead, her friends offered her a small part of her old life back in the form of an ordinary card game.

"How in the world can she play bridge?" I asked my father during my weekly phone call.

"She seems to recall the game, and your mother always was an intuitive player," he said.

"But remembering trump? And bidding signals?"

"She bids on impulse, not point count. She always did. She'll open on four points if she likes her cards. And who doesn't forget what's trump or whether they're on the board or in their hand? The Friends remind her."

Mom couldn't remember what day it was. She didn't know the month or year either. But the moment someone informed her it was Tuesday, she started in. "Where's my quar'er?" and, "Se' u' the car' table." As each job occurred to her—the quarter for the prize pot, the card table, three folding chairs, coffee, the good cups, four spoons, napkins, the good china plates—she barked orders. "Ha' a chee' san'wi' in wax paper on my pla'. Make the coffee. Na'kins on the table."

"Yes, yes, and yes. I told you I already did that," I'd assure her during summers and breaks when I helped with the set-up.

My mother oversaw preparations for the Tuesday games with an urgency that suggested she might forget if her orders weren't acted upon immediately. Of course, this was the case. To avoid a teary meltdown, hers mostly, I did whatever she asked when she asked.

With the table set and the coffee made, Mom rifled through her drawers for a booby prize, regifting from her stashes of soaps, lotions, candy—items worth more than the four quarters the winner would claim. There was no mistaking her pleasure when she won. Her grin said it all. If I was around, she handed the pot over to me with a "Here, Kath'een. Thi' i' for you."

"Thanks, Mom," I'd say and slip the four quarters into my pocket.

I never gave much thought to the mismatch between how she gave the money as if it was a hundred dollars, and the way I casually took her small gift. But she did not have access to money beyond the quarters given to her for bridge. I wish I'd realized at the time that when she gave me her winnings without hesitation, she was handing over to me all the money she had in the world.

More often than not, my mother lost at bridge. She always said she didn't mind because her friends could "u' the money for gasoline."

On Tuesdays after The Friends left and she had finished supervising the clean-up, she played Solitaire. It kept her mind occupied. Maybe. At least, she had something to do to pass the time until the next thing happened, whatever it was. She could not have said. And to the good, those games provided ideal conditions for winning, possibly even with an incomplete deck.

"Are you cheating?" I'd ask.

"Of cour'," she snapped, unable to hide her grin.

Once family and friends learned of Mom's cardplaying, decks of playing cards accumulated around the house. People gave them for birthdays and Christmas—souvenir decks with photos on the back, Bicycle cards from the dime store, and used decks from casinos at Lake Tahoe. Mom set aside the bridge sets for the weekly games and used the others for her endless games of Solitaire. One time while she was out, I counted fifty frayed decks in a drawer in her bedroom, many incomplete, some not sorted. No one was permitted to touch them much less throw them out.

Watching my mother retrieve a battered deck and play game after game of Solitaire intensified my longing to give her back her life, fill in all the gaps, be a hundred fifty percent the dutiful daughter. But I had another life as a student at Berkeley preoccupied with passing physics and protesting the war in Viet Nam, advocating for free speech, and marching for civil rights. I had plans to study abroad too. I didn't want to give any of this up. But I was often homesick and spent most weekends and those first two summers at home.

"Oh, Kath'een," my mother called out when she first spotted me. "Kath'een, Kath'een, come."

"Hi, Mom," I'd say.

"Oh, Kath'een, I'm so gla' you' here."

"Did you practice walking?"

"Ye'."

"Go to PT?"

"Ye'."

"Did you win at bridge?"

"No, I lo't."

"Did Kim bite anyone?"

"Watch ou'," she kidded.

She always laughed when I asked if she told Father Healy the joke about Holy Water, and then retold it.

Such were our conversations. I asked about something in her weekly schedule. And she answered, not with what really happened, but off the top of her head. She didn't always lose at bridge.

For all my longing to fill in the gaps, after we chatted and played a few games of Crazy Eights together, and I encouraged her to do her exercises, I left the house to visit friends or hang out at Judie's or locked myself away to study. I didn't help Dad with chores. I never gave a thought to my brother's loss or reached out to him.

Yet home offered me something that no other place could. Even short amounts of time spent in the bosom of my broken family took away the need to pretend. I didn't have secrets that set me apart. I belonged with the people most impacted by the terrible event that had happened, even though we didn't speak of it. Our different ways of adapting, like silence or absence, created tensions among us. But my mother's accident was never an elephant in the room.

As to the significance of the card games with The Friends, I arrived home in the middle of one of them after spending my junior year abroad. Dropping my suitcase in the entryway, I ran down the steps into the living room. My mother looked up at me from her hand, then back at her hand, then up at me again before she turned back to her partner. "Who' deal?" she asked.

I knew Mom loved me. Why hadn't she at least said hello? "Your mother wants to know when you are coming home," my father wrote in every one of his airletters to France. Stunned by her behavior, I struggled to make sense of it.

Without question, my mother's traumatic brain injury lay at the root of her dismissal and a lifelong lack of sentimentality. But her innate toughness was also factor, a quality she had in spades.

Chapter 13
Never Say Never

In August of 1970, a few weeks after my first wedding, my father had a heart attack. He retired a year later at age sixty-one. In spite of my mother's protests, he sold the house in the hills and bought a mobile home in Santa Cruz overlooking the ocean.

Just as the house in the hills was for my mother, my parents' new home at the beach was my father's dream come true, "tin box" though it was. The sea was in his blood. The son of a Dutch navigator, Dad had worked at the docks and on Dollar Line ships as a teenager. He also served in the Navy during WWII. "Next place you'll hit land is China," he said one day as he stood on his deck gazing out at the vast Pacific.

With Dad's retirement came changes. No more nurses. No housekeeper either. My father cooked, shopped, did the dishes and laundry, and cleaned. He also helped my mother bathe, but the bathroom was otherwise accessible for her needs. She made her bed, dressed herself. And she did her first and only "cooking" since her accident—a dip made of cottage cheese and dried Lipton Onion soup to accompany her nightly bourbon and water,

The heart attack that led to my father's premature retirement had caused severe damage, and he could not have taken the walks his doctor recommended at the old house in the hills. But he pushed Mom through the mobile home park every afternoon, Kim's leash tied to the wheelchair, stopping to chat with neighbors. Other than visits from family, their social life together centered primarily on these walks and monthly community potlucks.

One potluck night, my father was late getting back from a golf game. As he drove through the park, neighbors waved to him, more vigorously than usual, one gesturing almost frantically toward the clubhouse. When Dad arrived home to an empty house, he realized that the friendly waves weren't just to remind him of the potluck.

Apparently, Mom had gotten out of the walker she sat on to scoot around the house and crawled to the back door through the narrow space next to the washer and dryer. She made her way down the steps, pulled herself up into her wheelchair, and using her good leg, pushed herself uphill to the clubhouse with their permanent assignment of French bread and butter on her lap. She'd probably tossed them ahead of her as she made her way out of the house. Dad grinned. "I had to meet her over there."

For the first time since her accident, my mother had gone somewhere on her own. I had waited a long time for this thrilling I-told-you-so moment, prayed for it, willed it. Finally, I could let out the breath I'd been holding. Mom's old "let's go, hurry up" nature had resurfaced, proof to me that all those doctors were wrong. Never say never. She was still improving at ten years out.

Not long after my parents' move to the beach, my father joined an oil painting class as a favor to a neighbor who needed one more student to fill his class. A reader who loved poetry, Dad admitted he had never paid much attention to what things looked like, yet after one lesson, he fell in love with painting. To no one's surprise, he reinvented himself; to everyone's surprise, he chose painting. It consumed him. He built a studio off the living room, grew a beard, and took to wearing sandals and paint-spattered drawstring pants, and of course, a beret. Golf remained an interest, but as his ability to get around the course declined, his time at the easel increased.

"Now, which one do you like best?" he asked, every time I entered the house and then pointed out his most recent canvases propped on the floor in front of dozens of older paintings that lined the living room walls. While my mother played Solitaire, I listened to him talk about his work, the way I imagined she might have had she been able—the old roles and responsibilities muddled again.

Throughout my parents' fifteen years at the beach, even as my father's health declined, he made sure my mother got out of the house every day, no matter how tired he was. But my mother still resented staying home alone, whiling away hours playing Solitaire while he played golf, took classes, or painted. When he responded to her complaints, even with an "Oh, Dorothy," she would say, "Ju't pu' me in a home," referring to those nine months when he had. "Go ahea'. Ge' rid of me." She cut him no slack.

During a sabbatical in 1972, to take a little pressure off my father, I added a weekday to the regular weekend visits from my new husband and me and frequent drop-in visits from my brother who lived nearby. Every Thursday for a year, Mom and I went to lunch. I soon forgot the respite factor and looked forward to spending that time with her. We laughed a lot. "I ha' a hor'," she told me once at a restaurant on the Santa Cruz pier.

"How did you get a horse?" I asked, amazed at a never-before-told story.

"Someone ga' i' to me," she said. "I pu' i' in wi' the chi'ens."

"Good idea."

"Gram wa' very angry."

"Really?"

"Ye'," Mom laughed. "Her presus chi'ens."

"So you knew how much a girl can want a horse, and you still wouldn't get me one," I teased.

She gave me a look that said she stood by her "no money, no place to keep it" stance of long ago.

At another of our lunches, Mom told me The Friends had asked if I was planning to have children. "What did you say?" I asked. I'd been married a couple of years but had never mentioned anything one way or the other about children.

"I to' them you di'n't know how," she said, which I thought was very funny and a perfect way to end the questions.

In the fall of 1976, I drove over the hill to pay an unscheduled visit to my parents. I sat in Mom's walker facing Dad in his recliner and Mom on the couch. "I want you to know that I am fine and that I am getting a divorce," I began. My parents didn't seem surprised by my news. Although I hadn't shared any problems with them, maybe Mom had sensed them from the beginning. At my Summer Solstice wedding six years earlier, she interrupted the Universal Life minister as he stood in front of our hundred guests in full Huichol Indian garb. "Today is the longest day of the year," he began, at which point my mother called out," You ca' say tha' again."

Her comment to the end of my marriage was not among those I could have imagined either. "Tha's the bes' new' I've hea'd today," she said, before I could say more. Curious, I asked what other news she had heard that day.

"I ha' to ha' hemor'oi' su'ge'y."

On most visits to my parents', I stayed through dinner. Mom and I would shop for ingredients—that is, she rode along—and I would make a lasagna or chicken cacciatore, something my father might not make on his own. One time, just before I left after one of these meals, my mother invited my father to play their nightly cribbage game. He was lying back in his recliner, his eyes closed, the sound of his breathing loud in the room. He turned her down. My chest tightened as my mother smacked a deck against the table and began to deal anyway. I said goodbye and walked out the door not wishing to witness what happened next. My father followed me to my car. "Don't worry," he said. But how could I not? I worried about him all the time. And then he said something extraordinary. "When it's just the two of us, we're fine." At that instant, I experienced a rare moment of clarity and a profound sense of relief. He wasn't suggesting that my presence caused problems between them. He meant to reassure me. They were fine. They had a life together that I could neither imagine nor be a part of. It did not need me to mastermind it. This had never occurred to me, what with all the loss and change, what with all my ideas of how to improve things.

Another illuminating moment occurred when an old friend of my parents moved to the mobile park. I asked my father if he and Mom ever got together with her. The friend had been on the school board and a beach trip companion of Mom's too.

"Almost no one understands what your mother says. She isn't able to follow a conversation. This rules out socializing with our old friend and with other interesting residents of the park." He said this in an even objective way. Clearly, he didn't require intellectual stimulation from others or social interactions either to have a satisfying life. Painting, its history, and techniques, golf when he was well enough, the ocean, and simple routines sufficed. And my mother, of course, the love of his life.

But did I relax my vigilance? Of course not.

Part 3

Acceptance is a small quiet room.

Cheryl Strayed

Chapter 14
Over the Cliff

"I love you," I said to my father at the end of our weekly phone call. The following morning, he collapsed and was taken to the hospital by ambulance. Since his heart attack fifteen years earlier, trips to the hospital had multiplied. Miraculously, he returned home every time. But now things didn't look good. He'd been admitted to cardiac intensive care, unconscious.

I was eight months pregnant that hot July day in 1985 when the news of his collapse reached me in Southern California. For two years, I had been living there with Don, my second husband, and our almost-three-year-old daughter Laura. My little family flew back to the Bay Area immediately.

"I'm having contractions," I said to Don on the plane. "Good thing we're going to a hospital. I might need one."

"I want to see Grandpa," Laura whispered as we walked toward intensive care.

"You can't go in with me," I told her. "Grandpa's in a special room."

"I'm not afraid of rooms where Grandpa is," she said.

Inside the unit, I stood by Dad's bed. "Can you squeeze my hand?" I asked—the same question he had asked my mother throughout the months she lay unconscious. He squeezed but was otherwise unresponsive. Once I found out when the doctor would be with him the next day, Don, Laura, and I drove to the "tin box." Each time I returned to the hospital after that, my mother insisted I take the sports section of the paper, as she had during previous hospitalizations. Unable to realize this time was more serious, she didn't want to go herself. Or maybe she knew? During my father's days in a coma, I repeatedly assured him—as I had years earlier—that I'd take care of my mother, but the last thing I knew he heard for sure was my "I love you" over the phone.

On the fifth day after my father's collapse, a Tuesday, The Friends arrived at noon for the weekly bridge game. Barbara brought macaroni and cheese for our dinner. Don had taken Laura home to Southern California, so I retreated to the bedroom to sort through papers before driving to the hospital. While I was on the phone tending to some small matter, an operator interrupted the call, and my father's doctor came on the line to tell me my father had died without regaining consciousness. I went numb. I sat frozen in place for a few minutes, taking in shallow breaths and feeling the baby kick inside me. Then belly first, I pushed myself upright and took the first steps toward the living room, slowed more by the implications of my father's death than by my end-of-pregnancy waddle. As when I returned from a year in France and interrupted a card game, my mother's response was unpredictable and shocking. She looked up at me and then back at her friends. "Whose tu'n to p'ay?" she asked. As before, I'll never know whether I was witnessing strength or brain damage. But I believe that if I too disappeared from her life, she'd continue as always, uncomplaining and without a shred of self-pity, making the best of the cards she was playing at the time.

Not until the following evening did my mother say anything. We were driving home from a Chinese restaurant when she turned to me. "I can't belie' he's not here," she said. And not another word about Dad's death until twenty-five years later when she will ask me where he is. I don't remember her crying. But I didn't cry very much either. Perhaps the imminent birth of a new member of the family protected us some from the shock of our loss, kept me focused on the future, and the weight of new responsibilities. My mother was mine to look after now. No time to grieve. Many decisions to make quickly.

In the short time before returning home to give birth: I notified family and arranged for cremation. I contacted friends, former colleagues, and neighbors. From one, I received a quick tutorial in what must be done legally when someone dies and completed those tasks. I sorted through unpaid bills, wills, trusts, and conservatorship papers, deposited hundreds of dollars of checks I found tossed in a dresser drawer. I arranged a memorial service. On the same day, I petitioned the court to become my mother's conservator and replaced my parents' forty-year-old mattress, split in several places and leaking stuffing. I also hired an agency to oversee the live-in caregiver I had hired. She gave her notice the very day I arrived back at my mother's house four weeks later with an eleven-day-old infant cradled in my arms.

Don, our daughters, my step-kids, and I spent several weeks at a friend's beach house near Mom's place. I showed off baby Sarah to The Friends when they joined my mother for card games, prepared big family meals, and sorted through Dad's things, tossing some. I took the baby with me to court for the hearing at which I was named Mom's conservator. And I hired another caregiver figuring it was best for Mom to stay where she and Dad had lived and keep as much of her life as possible the same. The person I hired was the best of the applicants, and the agency would keep tabs on her. Fingers crossed, I returned home.

Two weeks later, just as I was getting the hang of managing with two children, Mom reported over the phone that her new caregiver left her alone for long stretches of time. What next? If I confronted the caregiver, would there be consequences for Mom? I badly wanted the arrangement to work. Maybe Mom had exaggerated or expected more from someone she was paying.

But she continued to complain about being left alone, and the grocery receipts the caregiver mailed to me each week—without the requested accounting—now included her cigarettes. I called her. She made excuses. I reduced my expectations.

Mom complained again. This time I traveled north. Mom's neighbor reported that he'd smelled marijuana and that a boyfriend spent a lot of time at the house. Confronted with this information, I faced the fact that I'd hired someone who needed a salary plus free room and board but felt no sense of obligation to care for my mother. I fired her.

The third caregiver was a former nurse and a dream. Involved in amateur theater, she took Mom to rehearsals. Outings around people, I thought! What could be better? But a few months into the job, this caregiver told me she couldn't handle the lack of intellectual stimulation that went along with tending to my mother.

She offered to oversee a new caregiver in exchange for staying on in her ocean view room rent-free. With this arrangement in place, I could finally relax.

Even better, the fourth caregiver, a part-time history professor at the community college, seemed sincerely to want the job. In my mind, I left Mom with a smart, responsible live-in person. And for a month, things went smoothly. Then late one Sunday night, I received a phone call from the overseer.

"Your mother's helper is behaving a little strangely."

I asked what she meant.

"She told me she's being promoted to chair of her department."

"Isn't that good news?" I asked.

"She's obsessing about the name plate on her office door, about changing it."

"On her own? Just changing the nameplate?"

"Well, I have a friend at the college and as far as she knows, the chair of the department has no intention of leaving."

"Is she crazy?" I asked, alarmed.

"Hard to say. She does seem paranoid. It's possible she's on meds and forgot to take them. I'll get back to you tomorrow."

I trusted the overseer to handle the situation.

In her call the next day though, she told me the professor had thrown away everything in the house made of plastic. Enough. I had to go north again. But before I'd completed travel arrangements, the professor backed Mom's car off a cliff thirty feet to the rocks below with my mother on the front seat next to her. The accident made the front page of the local paper, photo above the fold. "She must have gunned it," a policeman told me. The caregiver had walked away. My mother sustained a broken leg and a concussion. She spent the next month in a skilled nursing facility.

The agency had failed. Three caregivers failed. The one-time caregiver living in the house to oversee the new help hadn't been able to prevent a terrible outcome. Clearly, I couldn't manage the situation from Southern California. And since Don owned a Rose Parade Float business, we had to live near Pasadena. I gave up on the notion of Mom staying on at the beach. After her leg healed, I brought her to live with me.

Within a few months of Mom's arrival, Don found a job in San Francisco, and we moved back to the Bay Area not far from The Friends. The family, my mother especially, had been through a rough couple of years. But as anyone who has tried multi-generational living could have predicted—our ages spanned fifty years—or lived with five people in a two-bedroom house (eight people in the summer when my step-kids visited), or cared for a brain-injured person, the hard times were not behind us.

Chapter 15
The Gift of a Crumb

Picture this. My mother and I are at the dinner table in our Northern California home, me with a million to-dos on my mind—all equally important, of course, and all related to the needs of others as I've determined them—proof of how good a daughter, mother, wife, friend, and teacher I am. The girls have left the table to do homework. Don is in Phoenix on business. Mom finishes stacking all the dirty dishes within reach onto her plate ignoring my orders not to. She has one thing on her mind. The same thing every night. I brace myself when I stand to take our empty plates to the kitchen.

"Se'…" she says.

"Yes, I know. Set the table for breakfast at night."

"Kath'een, se' the table for brea'fas' at ni'," she says, as I disappear into the kitchen.

"Good idea, Mom," I say, clenching my teeth and swishing the forks in soapy water. She wants to help, to share one thing she remembers doing when she had kids and a husband and a demanding job. She doesn't remember giving this same advice year in and year out for a dozen years. She's going to keep repeating it too. If I don't do what she asks instantly, she'll forget.

"Kath'een."

I stall. "I *will* set the table tonight," I tell her in a loud voice, so she'll be sure to hear me, and repeat my promise, upping the volume. Shouting feels surprisingly good. But promises are never enough.

I slip the plates in the dishwasher.

"Oh, Kath'een. Come. Come."

"I will. I am. Almost done, Mom." I drop the utensils in their caddies. Handles up or handles down? Which is the right way? Why don't I know? Why didn't she tell me before she lost her mind?

"Mom," my older daughter calls. "Can you come here?"

"No, I can't," I shout. "You'll have to wait."

"Kath'een," my mother calls again.

I move to where she can see me, force a smile and wave a soapy cooking fork. This feels surprisingly good too. Then I return to the sink and cram the glasses on the designated rack where they don't quite fit.

"Kath'een, Kath'een, Kath-eeeen."

Now, there's a hysterical urgency in her voice. I slam the pot I'm washing into the dish pan. Water splashes onto the floor. Again, I return to the table. "Mom," I say, with an edge. "Can you just wait a second? I'm busy."

"Oh, Kath'een." Her voice drops off into a sob.

Inside me, the familiar fight rages on: *Why can't she just let me finish?—Because she can't.—Why can't she wait for once? —Because she can't.—Why can't she realize she's not helping me?—She is unable.—I get my hands wet then dry them only to get them wet again.—Big deal. Her request is a simple one after all.—But how many times must I leave and return to the sink tonight? Is it too much to want to load the dishwasher first? Will I ever be able to finish anything I start, without her interruptions? Or will she have yet another suggestion for making my life easier?*

Exhaling, I dry my hands on a dishtowel. She watches me lay out full place settings around the table. I turn the glasses upside down, so they won't get dust in them overnight. She demands this. I have explained to her many times that I have only toast and coffee for breakfast and don't need utensils or glasses—more times than it would take a quicker learner to figure out that the job needs to be done to her specifications as soon as she asks—and just do it.

But I am not a quick learner, and sometimes I have other things on my mind like the third graders I'll face in the morning. Sometimes, I don't want to set the table at night. Sometimes, I simply want to do things my way. I want a life too.

Once the table is set, she stops crying. Have I lost another battle? Won it? Is battle even the right word? The scene is over, and that's good. Once again, I've ended it the only way possible—by giving in. Does this cost me something?

Multiply the scenario by thousands over decades.

"Kath'een, come," when I was a high school studying for a math test, "Kath'een" during college breaks when I wanted to sleep in, while I was playing backgammon with my new husband, or changing a diaper, brushing my teeth, basting a turkey, talking on the phone, writing a check, or reading the newspaper.

"Kath'een, Kath'een, Kath'een."

She couldn't even pronounce the name she gave me.

Before I finished loading the dishwasher, the phone rang. It was my mother's tax accountant with the answer to a question. I wrote down the information.

"You're lucky you still have your mother," the accountant said. "I lost mine."

I resisted the urge to explain that I was my mother's mother, that she needed care, that I was motherless.

"You're very lucky," the accountant repeated. "No one will ever love you like your mother."

"Well—" I began.

"Or annoy you as much either," she interrupted. "This is true too."

"Complicated," I said, and hung up the phone.

Flashing her gap-toothed grin, my mother rolled toward me until her wheelchair was wedged between the wall and a dining room chair. "Here, Kath'een. I ha' somethin' for you." She held out her hand, thumb and forefinger closed on a crumb she picked up off the floor.

"Thanks, Mom," I said, forcing another smile. For a moment, I was able to accept how things are and put aside how I'd like them to be.

She released the crumb into my open palm and watched while I carried her offering directly to the trash. She only wants to help. And I want to be the good daughter she deserves. I want to be the good mother, the good wife, and the good teacher too. And I'm failing. I'm failing at everything.

Chapter 16
One Hat Too Many

The thud of the BarcaLounger jolting upright followed by my husband's rapid footsteps telegraphs his level of concern. He sprints into the kitchen. Wide-eyed and silent, my blond daughters, six and nine years old, stare at me over their bowls of Cheerios. Hunched in her wheelchair sobbing, my mother kicks at the floor with her left foot, in the effort to back away from the table.

I had snapped again.

"What happened?" Don asks, as he takes in the scene in the kitchen.

"Mom threw the microwave at the wall," Laura says in a frightened voice.

"Actually," I correct. "I shoved it off the counter, and it hit the wall. Mom spilled *again*. OK?" I go on. "Every night I tell her the same thing, 'Don't stack the dishes.' Then she does anyway."

"I wa' to he'p'," my mother says, still crying as she maneuvers her wheelchair toward her bedroom. "I wa' to he'p you."

"You only make more work for me," I say. "Please don't help."

My husband looks me in the eye. "You need medication," he says.

Not a millisecond of satisfaction is gained from my increasingly frequent outbursts. Stretched too thin, I lose it over some little thing and then aim my anger at the easiest target, my mother, even when she isn't the cause. The outbursts are forcing my poor blameless mother to feel like a burden—the last thing she wants to be to her daughter—and even more, they are destroying my marriage and frightening my children. Yet ashamed as I am, I can't stop. My husband's advice about meds hits home. I need an instant and radical change of consciousness.

At the psychiatrist's, I use the term "murderously angry." She prescribes a powerful tranquillizer. For several weeks, I lie around on the couch in a bovine state. When I can focus at all, I chew on what brought me to the brink of a breakdown.

I think about the Christmas cards I sent when I was sixteen and the holiday meals I prepared in an attempt to fill the hole my mother left when she disappeared from her place in the family—all the ways I tried to fix our family, to make up for what was missing.

And here I am twenty-five years later, still at it. My father died, and I am trying to compensate for his absence by having my mother live with me and by arranging stimulating activities she'll enjoy—a senior day program, luncheons for her bridge group, swim therapy sessions.

But my father had only to exist to give my mother's life meaning and purpose. And it is not within my power to make up for the loss of him or any of her other unfathomable losses. Besides, I am going crazy trying.

After four years of living with my mother, my "I-can-do-this, bring-it-on" approach has left me exhausted, frustrated, and finally uncontrollably angry. And it has resulted in failure. I cannot care for my mother and provide companionship and keep the rest of my life going—teach school, be a wife and a mother—much less do all this alone during the six months of the year when my husband travels.

By the time I stop taking the meds and get up off the couch, I have pretty much decided to stop caring for my mother in my home. My life will be less stressful. I'll be able to give my daughters and husband the attention they deserve. Perhaps I'll even have a few minutes for myself. Most importantly, I won't kill anyone.

I take my mother to see the new assisted living facility two blocks from our house. "This is where you'll stay when Don and I and the kids go to Boston," I tell her, referring to our upcoming trip to one of my step-kids' graduations. I do not tell her that she will not live with us when we return. I haven't yet fully admitted it to myself.

She looks around the sunlit lobby decorated with plants and white wicker furniture. Residents relax and doze on soft couches upholstered in muted floral patterns.

"Nothing here bu' a bunch of goddamned ol' people," she says.

Part 4

When I understand that the glass is already broken,
every moment with it is precious.

Achaan Chaa

Chapter 17
Isn't It Wonderful?

In assisted living, my mother had a studio apartment on the ground floor that looked out on an oak tree. Aides helped her bathe and dispensed her thyroid pills. She used the bathroom, dressed and undressed, and wheeled herself to meals independently. She was able to work her TV—it had a simple on/off switch and manual dial for changing channels—and watched reruns of her favorite old shows on weekday afternoons. She made herself a bourbon and water before dinner and had it with crackers and her simple dip of cottage cheese and dehydrated onion soup. She was unable to master the microwave, but there was no need.

Four days a week, Mom attended her senior day program. The Friends showed up on Tuesdays for lunch and bridge. I visited by myself and with the kids, as did my husband, and we often brought her to the house. My mother was the most independent she'd been since the accident, and I actually think she enjoyed it.

Yet at first, the kids kept asking when Grandma was coming home. The Friends asked why I sent her away. My mother asked if she could live with me again. She promised not to be any trouble and pointed out that we would save money. Did I feel guilty? Was I being selfish? Might there have been other solutions? Yes, yes, and yes.

Although placing my mother in assisted living lightened my load, I was still on call—and the only one on call—for everything. More than once, I'd been asked to deal with behaviors I though the staff should handle. For instance, the night they called to inform me, "Your mother took a purse someone left in the lobby. She said she didn't, but we know she did. Will you come and get it from her?"

Hoping to avoid getting dressed and making the trip, I telephoned my mother and asked if she had the purse.

"No," she said.

"Mom, someone saw you take it," I explained. "Please don't make me come over. It's late."

"I don' ha' i'," she said.

"Yes, you do," I insisted and then said the words I knew would make her comply. "Please don't make my life harder."

"It di'n' belon' to anyone," she retorted.

"They're coming to get it," I said. "Return it."

Mom returned the purse.

But as she entered her eighties and age compounded her physical problems, the calls became more frequent and serious. One Saturday morning not long after the move, I was at the kitchen counter slicing oranges into quarters for halftime snacks when the phone rang. The girls were gobbling the last of their Honey Nut Cheerios, Laura in a turquoise soccer jersey, her straight blond hair pulled back into ponytail, and Sarah in lime green, her blond curls tucked into French braids. Don was reading the Chronicle and drinking coffee. The call was from my mother's assisted living facility. She had fallen out of her wheelchair and possibly broken her leg. Would I come right away?

"Yes, of course. I can be there in ten minutes," I answered.

Don peered out from behind his paper.

"They think Mom broke her leg," I told him, then added, "Maybe it's not…," my feeble attempt to smooth over what a broken leg might mean for her, for all of us.

"Is Grandma OK?" Laura asked.

"She'll be fine," I assured her. "You know Grandma."

"Are you going to miss my game?" Sarah asked.

"Mom will catch up with us later if she can," Don told the kids. "After she checks on Grandma."

I arrived just after the paramedics. Lying helpless on the floor in the middle of her studio apartment, Mom was in high spirits in spite of the crisis, rising to the occasion as she always did and clearly enjoying the attention of the three good-looking young guys hovering over her.

I was not in high spirits, having just let go of watching the girls play soccer and chatting with friends on the dew-damp sidelines. I was in the throes of bidding farewell to what I thought I might be doing for the rest of the day, not to mention the week, month, and possibly the better part of the year. Once again. Would life ever be easier? Or smoother? Or uneventful? Or boring?

With my mother, things came up—this was her *second* broken leg and the tip of an iceberg of incidents that required my presence. As fast as future plans faded, concerns about living arrangements and the cost of additional caregiving replaced them.

"Oh, Kath'een," my mother called from the floor "I'm so gla you're here. Isn't it won'erfu' I bro' my leg on Saturday?"

Before I had a chance to respond, one of the EMTs asked Mom if she could use her good leg to help them get her up from floor to a chair and then to the gurney.

"No," I intervened, as I had countless times in doctors' offices and explained that she was partially paralyzed and unable to walk.

After determining that Mom indeed broke her leg, but nothing else, the team lifted her gently off the floor and settled her on the gurney, postponing the inevitable neurological evaluation until they'd strapped her in place.

I'd been at her side during many of these exams, watched her forehead wrinkle and eyes turn up in concentration as she attempted to retrieve what she thought she should know from her damaged brain. She had never come within decades of naming a sitting president or of stating her own age. She did not know where she lived. However, her "poor memo'y" as she called it, did not prevent her from feeling humiliated.

"She won't be able to answer any of your questions," I informed the crew. "She hasn't been able to answer them for almost forty years," I added, in a voice tinged with residual anger at life's injustices, then launched into a tirade as if Mom weren't there. "And that's not all. She can't tell you what happened this morning either, for that matter, or what she had for breakfast."

Catching myself, I continued in a calmer voice. "This is normal, her baseline, her current mental state," I said. "Trust me."

The gorgeous EMT with the clipboard locked his big blue eyes on me. "I'm sorry, ma'am. We have procedures, and we're..."

"Stop right there," I said, staring back. "You'll have to trust me."

He shook his head but after a nod from one of his companions, let the clipboard fall to his side.

Their checklist complete—with the one exception—the crew wheeled my mother out of the building as I followed behind. "Isn't i' lucky I bro'my leg on Saturday?" she called to me. "I'm so gla' I bro'my leg on Saturday," she said as they hoisted her into the back of the ambulance. "Isn't it good I bro' my leg on Saturday?" she repeated as a paramedic placed the blood pressure cuff on her arm. "I'm so lucky. Don can ta' care of the children."

I climbed into the front seat of the ambulance. Even though Mom was right about Don and the girls, I just couldn't consider the timing of any broken leg good luck. As the driver pulled out of the parking lot, the other attendant relayed from the back, "120 over 60. Pressure of a twenty-year-old."

"Her usual," I commented. "Take mine if you want to see some high numbers."

As the paramedics unloaded my mother at Stanford Hospital, she thanked them for the lovely music they played for her on the short ride, then turned to me. "It's Saturday, Kath'een. Isn't tha' won'erfu'?"

I said nothing.

We spent the better part of the day waiting since she was not experiencing chest pain, a surefire way to be seen immediately in an ER.

"I'm so gla' I bro' my leg on Saturday," she kept repeating in the waiting room.

"Mom," I finally said. "I don't think it's so great you broke your leg on Saturday. I don't think it's so great you broke your leg at all."

Unable to remember what she'd just said, she continued to comment on her good fortune throughout the day.

As I had anticipated, an ER doctor confirmed my mother would need more assistance than the care facility could provide. I called around and found a spot for her starting the next day in one of the area's finer skilled nursing facilities, located a mile from the hospital. Stanford agreed to keep her overnight in a small observation room off the ER. Anxious to return home and check in with the kids about their games, I left Mom before she moved to her room.

"See you later," I told her. "I'll be back after dinner."

But moments after I reached home, the phone rang. "Kath'een, come. Come ba'. You ha' to see the view ou' my wi'dow. Come. You ha' to come now."

I didn't have the heart to say no. She was too excited and happy.

And so, while the sun was still shining, I drove back to the hospital. The window of her room faced the ER parking lot. I had to look twice to see what she meant by lovely view. "Yes," I told her when I spotted the tree. "I agree. Lovely." At the center of the asphalt lot stood a symbol, if ever there was one, of strength and endurance—an aged oak tree with a massive, deeply-furrowed trunk and a broad, rounded, shade-giving canopy.

The frugal gene runs strong in our family. My mother's cousin Charlie drove his embalmed mother to the cemetery in the back of the van he used in his gardening business rather than pay for a hearse. So on the morning of Mom's discharge from the hospital, I decided to save the $400 cost of an ambulance and drive her the mile to the nursing facility. She could recline on the padded floor of our van, her splinted leg stretched out in front of her. She would approve of this money-saving move and would be game to ride that way. My husband, on the other hand, disapproved of the scheme and refused to participate, so I enlisted the help of the two aides who accompanied us out of the ER.

"It's the white van," I said, pointing. "Just put her in back on the floor."

"Uhh, we're not supposed to...," said the aide with the man-braids.

"I'm pretty sure regulations won't allow us," his companion added, staring down at his Nikes.

"Look," I said. "An ambulance will cost $400 for a one-mile ride."

At that, they stopped hemming and hawing, rolled Mom up next to the sliding door, and hefted her into the van.

Once in the driver's seat, I took a moment to fix in memory the few minutes before the "illegal" transfer. I had wheeled my mother past the busy nursing station. Mom waved to the nurses and called out. They continued scribbling in their charts. Mom insisted we stop. She repeated what she'd said, but the nurses looked at her puzzled, so I translated her garbled speech, filling in the consonants she couldn't pronounce. The nurses burst out laughing and were still smiling and wishing her well when we rolled on.

My mother had said, "Goodbye. Thank you. I had a wonderful time."

The thing was, for her, it was true.

Chapter 18
Italy? Really?

Years ago, after spending a summer studying Spanish in Spain, I met up with my parents in Italy. My father, then seventy and suffering from congestive heart failure, wanted to visit art museums. He had been painting for a decade and had studied and copied the great masters of the Renaissance, Titian a favorite.

So visit art museums we did. Awestruck, he wandered through the Uffizi Gallery and the Pitti Palace, gazing in rapture at entire walls of paintings he'd only seen in books. My mother glanced at the art but seemed more interested in other tourists. We also visited the town where my grandmother was born. The relatives offered us huge meals that featured regional specialties like truffles and Barolo wine. We explored the church with the blue ceiling and gold stars that my grandmother remembered from childhood. Next, we traveled to Venice where Italian friends dubbed my father Papa 'emingway, struck by his full white beard and long curly white hair. I was Katerina, tall and thin with wild reddish-brown curls, and my mother, in photos always seated in her wheelchair between the two of us, straw sun visor pulled low, was Dorotee, pronounced just the way Uncle Vincent did.

Fast forward to my bright idea when my mother turned seventy-nine. Why not repeat this wonderful trip?

"Are you nuts?" one of my friends asked, then added unkindly, "Would you take a three-year-old to Italy?" Even if Mom's mental age tested in the single digits, she had lived a long life, rich in challenges and rewards, some of which she remembered. Besides, her injured brain was still capable of experiencing pleasure. I wished to provide an opportunity. Mom deserved to go to Italy again, and my father would have taken her if he had been able. But he was gone, and I was responsible for her now—for the quality of her life—where she lived, the clothes she wore, her hair styles, her outings and activities. In full high-horse mode, I wanted to do as fine a job as my father would have, or better. I hadn't given up wanting her to have the life she deserved or at least a little of the one she might have had.

"Won'erfu', won'er'fu'," Mom said when I proposed the trip.

I signed us up for a two-week tour designed for people in wheelchairs. Don would take care of our preteen daughters. For sixteen days, I would focus on my mother and have a vacation of sorts too. I would not be responsible for the girls' lives— my high horse operating at a full gallop there as well.

You might guess that the moment the tour for the disabled was cancelled, I dropped plans to go to Italy. But no, I decided to go ahead. After all, I was perfectly capable of taking my mother on my own and even spoke passable Italian. It'll be fun, I thought, and went about booking flights, accessible rooms, and arranging to rent a car at the airport in Milan that would accommodate the wheelchair.

On a sunny mid-October day, Mom and I took off for Italy. We must have been somewhere over the Atlantic when my husband accidentally maxed out our credit card. Twenty hours later, navigating the crowds at the Milan airport, I found the car rental office. "Sorry, no car," the clerk said.

"What do you mean, no car?" I said. "I reserved one with a trunk big enough for my mother's wheelchair."

"Sorry, Signora. No car."

"I don't understand."

"No money, no car," he said, showing me his empty palms.

"But I gave you my credit card."

"No good." He shrugged his shoulders, shook his head, and waved his hand in the air. "No money. No car. Nothing I can do."

I asked to borrow the phone and made a trans-Atlantic call to my husband, my mother's refrain in the background, "Kath'een, Kath'een, let's go."

"We're at the car rental agency at the Milan airport," I told him, unable to disguise my extreme annoyance. "Mom wants to leave the airport now." I held out the phone so he could hear her. "There's a problem with the credit card, and they won't give me the car I reserved. Fix this." But he never could. Something about waiting for reimbursement for his business travel expenses. I carried back-up traveler's checks but not enough to cover all our expenses—starting with the big rental car. The uncertainty over whether the card would work plagued us right up until our flight home.

Just as I was about to scream or cry, the clerk said, "Maybe we have something for you for less money."

I couldn't decide whether to kiss or kick him. He might have mentioned this possibility before I reached meltdown. But I was so relieved to have a car, I just filled out the paperwork and left.

Twenty-three hours into the trip, jet-lagged, and sleep-deprived, Mom and I were finally cruising at high speed—is there any other on an autostrada—toward Verona in a tiny red Fiat, wheelchair jammed into the hatchback. My map showed that our hotel was near the Verona train station, but after creeping along nearby narrow streets, exploring others that radiated from a square, and backing up a one-way street in an attempt to locate a street sign, I couldn't find it. I gave up and pulled into the station parking lot, got out, and spread a map on the hood of our car. As I tried to make sense of it, a kind Italian man stopped, and instead of explaining how to get to our hotel, led us there in his car through a maze of thoroughfares and one-way streets. Only in Italy.

A glance at our hotel room revealed it was not accessible. Mom would not be able to get into to the bathroom without help. This meant waking up with her multiple times that night. I suggested we go to bed.

"Wha' ti' is it?" Mom asked.

"Six-thirty," I told her. "We've been up for twenty-four hours."

"It's dinner ti'," she said. "I wan' dinner."

"Italians don't eat dinner at 6:30," I said.

"I do," she said.

"Are you hungry?"

"It's dinner ti'."

So I crammed her wheelchair back into the tiny elevator, transferred her to the car, stowed the chair, and took off toward the center of town. By then it was raining. Leaving her in the car, I scouted several restaurants, all closed until later.

"I'll take you back to the hotel and get take-out from a restaurant nearby," I said, stifling an "I told-you-so."

As we headed for the hotel, it started to rain buckets—*piovere a catinelle* in Italian. The narrow curved streets of the old city filled with bumper-to-bumper cars as the evening commute ratcheted up. In the heavy downpour, I could barely see the taillights on the car in front of me. I was afraid to stop. I couldn't see what was on either side. In my foggy state, I decided to just keep following the car ahead until the traffic and rain subsided.

"Whe' a' we?" my mother asked.

Where are we? I paused to ponder how to answer this frequent question. Italy was a possible answer, maybe the obvious one for Mom. Or Verona. Downtown? Or the truth? That I didn't know where we were. I opted for the truth.

"A' leas' you know whe' ou' ho'el is," my mother said.

At that moment, I realized the breadth of our predicament. "But I don't know where the hotel is," I said. I hadn't been able to find the hotel earlier, and conditions had worsened. "And Mom, I don't even remember the name of it."

At this she burst out laughing. What else was there to do? I joined her.

"Stop," she said, barely able to speak. "I ha' to go to the ba'room."

But where to stop and how? A gas station? Oh my God, an Italian gas station! Familiar with my mother's habits, I knew we had only minutes to find a toilet. I managed to detach the Fiat from the amoebic traffic pattern that had swept us up. Shall I mention that the toilet was Turkish style, two footprints in the middle of an enamel basin on the floor? My mother couldn't squat, but she couldn't wait either. I'll spare you the details.

Back in the car, I suddenly remembered sticking a card with the name of the hotel on the dashboard. Relieved, we set out again, locating our destination in a mere hour.

"You sure you still want dinner?" I asked once we were back in our room. But I already knew the answer. "I'll be right back with food," I said. "You wait here."

I found a pizzeria and ordered a pizza with porcini, her favorite mushroom. While I was waiting, a waiter started up a conversation. In broken Italian, I told him about our failed trip to get dinner—the rain, the closed restaurants, the traffic, being lost.

"Well then, you had a fine tour of the city," he said in an upbeat tone.

I instantly adopted this quintessentially Italian spin on my tale of misery. Italy! No place like it. Yes, a fine tour. Mom even loved the pizza although she insisted there weren't any mushrooms on it.

The following morning, we set out for Lake Garda, only an hour away. You might think what I remember about our visit there would be the bronze and gold of autumn leaves on the trees framing a view of the crystal-clear water, or Castello Scaligero, or the gnocchi in gorgonzola sauce with fresh truffles? But no. What made the trip memorable was the chocolate gelato cone I bought for my mother. Even with the fistful of napkins I grabbed, I couldn't keep up with the drips and splashes as it melted far faster than she could lick.

After the first alarming, "Oh, Kath'een," I gave up keeping up. There was no controlling the spectacular dark brown mess on her face and hands, on her clothes and in the car. We'll use a towel later, I told her. Meanwhile, she laughed and licked with nary a glance at the lake.

Accessibility dictated our itinerary, and I'd booked us into a hotel in the spa town of Abano Terme, a stop on the canceled tour. Again, the room was not accessible—none on the trip were—but at least there was a pool of hot water to look forward to after a day of pushing Mom's wheelchair over cobblestones, figuring out where and what to eat, dealing with restrooms, Italian signage and parking.

On my way back to our room after my first soak, I picked up a few tourist brochures, one advertising the beauty of the nearby Euganean Hills. I learned what Shelley wrote about them.

> Beneath is spread like a green sea
> The waveless plain of Lombardy,
> Bounded by the vaporous air,
> Islanded by cities fair—

Petrarch too described the beauty of the area. "Slopes clothed with vines and olives." I'd never heard of the Euganean Hills, but the ease of a drive through beautiful countryside and a stress-free stroll in an estate garden appealed.

And what a garden it turned out to be with a hundred yards of descending pools set into a gently sloping hillside and fed by cascades, a manicured hedge maze, and statuary throughout. But what struck me most as I pushed Mom along the broad raked paths was the feathery texture of the landscaping, planted over the 500 years the garden had existed—layers of green from medieval evergreens framing manicured beds of perennials, the only splash of color from startlingly white impatiens surrounding a gurgling fountain. I'm not sure what Mom thought of the garden. She didn't say much, not the next day either when we drove to Padua to see the Giotto frescos and then on to Sienna where we had our best meal—scampi with biscotti and sweet wine for dessert. We had our second-best meal on a Sunday afternoon at one of those roadside inns, its full carpark an excellent clue to the quality of the food.

Later I'd be asked if my efforts to create the trip of a lifetime were worthwhile. Would my mother even remember the trip? Until the drive to Rome, our final destination, I have to admit I questioned my sanity many times. But my lasting memory is of my mother staring out the car window, watching the scenery scroll by—small, white-washed villages atop rolling green hills, a church at the center of each, its spire reaching skyward. She never took her eyes off the beautiful Italian landscape, as if she felt a connection to where generations of her family had

lived their lives, as if some part of her was home. Transfixed
and deeply content, she gazed with the same quality of attention she watched fires in our fireplace back in Palo Alto. I knew
the trip had been worth taking, and we hadn't even arrived in
Rome.

As it turned out, Mom didn't see Rome, just the insides of two hotel rooms, the first near the Vatican, where she became ill. I con-
fess to leaving her alone and making a guilty visit to St. Peter's.

Then after a wretched night, the only night I could reserve,
I stripped her bed and bundled the soiled linens while she
pleaded non-stop for me to just leave her in Italy. "Ta' me to a
ho'pi'al, an' go ho' to the children," as if she knew that what I
feared most was her ending up in an Italian hospital with me at
her bedside and never seeing my children again.

During three nights at a pricy airport hotel—credit card
accepted—Mom recovered enough to fly. I had decided in Pa-
dova to shorten our trip, returning home a few days earlier
than originally planned. But with her illness and an eight-hour
delay at the Rome airport—two hours on the tarmac and six
more hours back in the gate area—and a missed connecting
flight from New York to California that required another night
in a hotel, we arrived home on the day of our original return.

"I wen' to Italy," she told The Friends and recounted her
single lasting memory. It was of the two of us lost in the rain-
storm and not knowing the name or location of our hotel. Each
of the many times she told the story, she laughed as hard as she
had that night in Verona.

A month after our return, when I had more or less recovered, I kiddingly asked her where she would like to go next.

"Ge'ma'y," she said, without hesitation.

And for a split second, I considered it.

Chapter 19
Expect the Unexpected

When my mother could no longer move from her bed to her chair safely, I hired twenty-four-hour care in the hope she could live out her life in her apartment with the view of the old oak tree. For two years, a series of kind Tongan women cared for her, but this arrangement proved too costly. It was time for the final move.

Dread overcame me as the day approached, the signal my mother was heartbreakingly close to the end of the line. At skilled nursing, she would lose the last shreds of normailty—wicker furniture in a light-filled room and using the bathroom when needed, not at the convenience of staff. Diapering is routine in nursing homes and no matter how many conversations I had with the director of nursing about offering Mom access to a toilet, she refused.

I had broken my leg when I slipped and fell on a hike shortly before moving day, so my mother and I rolled into her new accommodations in our respective wheelchairs. "Are you a new resident too?" a young aide asked me, an unpleasant reminder that my own end of the line wasn't as remote as I liked to believe.

Under the pall of Mom's new losses, I couldn't find an up-side to her move. Stalked by guilt—after all, it should have been to my house—I watched as she adapted to the change the way she always had, making the best of her new situation.

She prowled the halls picking up trash and turning off lights "to sa' electricity," and to the annoyance of the staff, watering plants to death. She attended every activity—news of the day discussions, exercise, singing, and games. She even crashed staff meetings where they tell me she nods and shuffles handouts like the regular participants.

Well into their eighties, The Friends stopped coming to play cards soon after the move. So one Tuesday shortly after I retired, I kicked off a new tradition to make that day of the week special.

At noon, I find my mother in the corridor outside the room she shares with three others. A split second after she spots me, recognition then relief spread across her face as if I'd been lost, and she found me again. No one is ever as happy to see me as my mother. "Oh, Kath'een, Kath'een," she says, her face relax-ing into her broad, open-mouthed grin. "I'm so gla' you're he'. Oh, boy. I'm so lucky. Whe' a' we goin'?"

Despite losing more of her memory to old age, one thing she does retain is that my arrival signals an outing. And even if I felt oppressed by other responsibilities, I soon find myself as pleased as she is. Her enthusiasm is contagious. For all her excitement, we might well be going to Paris or Rome or Ger-many.

We hold hands for a moment. Hers is soft and warm. There's a scratch on the back and dry blood where her fragile skin split. She won't be able to tell me what happened. As she puts it, "I ha' a ve'y poo' memo'y."

"We're going on a picnic," I tell her, careful not to mention what day it is. If I inadvertently name it, she'll tell me that she can't go because "The Frie'ds a' coming." The old routine is etched in her long-term memory. For her brain to lay down a new path, it would take the neural equivalent of the westward movement. If I happen to slip up and mention Tuesday, I'll have to tell a lie that relieves her anxiety and leaves her free to come with me. "The Friends canceled."

As to those card games with The Friends, I can't banish my lingering regret they couldn't go on forever. They were important to me too. During those two hours a week when my mother was immersed in her old life, I couldn't make her a single bit happier.

Before we can leave for our picnic, Mom insists I check the top drawer of her bedside table. There she stores the gifts she's saved for me, the detritus of her circumscribed world: individual packets of jam, sugar, syrup, or mayonnaise—a few partly open and oozing; a stuffed animal or two from bingo; pens she's swiped; the occasional book; stale, crumbled cookies in plastic bags labeled with her name and room number, sneaked out of the dining room under the cushion of her wheelchair; magazine coupons; a leaflet or songbook from the Sunday church service; single serving boxes of breakfast cereal, and seasonal holiday decorations—most recently an American flag from the on-site Fourth of July picnic.

"Thanks, Mom," I say, as she hands over her booty. "Very thoughtful."

"Hi' them, Kath'een," she whispers.

I drop a cereal box into my purse and slip packets of condiments in my pocket. We conceal the potted artificial flower and small stuffed monkey in the daypack she always keeps with her. When she's not looking, I throw away the muffin haphazardly wrapped in a napkin and already leaking crumbs.

It has taken more years than I like to admit before I finally got it and stopped telling her that I couldn't use all that cereal or that the children were grown, gone, and no longer interested in stuffed animals. Likewise, it took far too long for me to stop asking her where she had obtained the items in her top drawer. I knew, and she knew I knew. She'd admit to winning a few items at the weekly bingo game but otherwise ignored my attempts to make her reconsider her klepto habit.

Still, I am touched by these tokens of her love and concern and find it hard to throw them out, even the bright orange, shaggy-haired, google-eyed stuffed monster she recently passed on to me. In one of the few ways she is able, she is still taking care of me. However, the day she tried to give me a wallet—abandoned near a chair in the library, she said—I insisted that we return it.

On this first Tuesday, after we are all packed up, she gazes up at me from her wheelchair. "Kath'een, wha' sha' I do now?"

"We're going out," I shout. "Picnic."

She won't wear her hearing aids. During our card games, we sometimes use the mic with earphones I bought. Her face transforms from passive to alert and inquisitive when she can hear again. But after a few short exchanges of the usual patterned sort, she pulls off the earphones "to sa' the ba'eries."

"Oh, boy," she says, as I roll her toward the car. "Thi' i' won'erfu'."

The transfer from chair to car is complicated by her terror of falling and inability to trust anyone.

"Have I ever dropped you?" I ask, unable to suppress waves of exasperation after 10,000 safe transfers. "Have I ever?" I ask again.

"I don' know," she answers truthfully. "Ho' me, ho' me, ho' me," she cries as I ease her into the front seat of the car. Loss of muscle control and balance from her brain injury are now compounded by age and further atrophy, her joints worn to near uselessness.

I'm about to heft her wheelchair and daypack into the trunk. But she wants help with her seatbelt the instant she's seated and starts to cry. She can't wait until after I finish loading and take my place behind the wheel, so I leave the chair by the trunk, clamp my lips shut, and lean over her to secure her seatbelt. Then I load the chair and get in.

After she's settled with her battered Kleenex box containing comb, brush, used and unused tissues beside her, we're almost ready to leave. "Is my whee'cha' in the ca'?" she asks anxiously.

"Yes, Mom," I say. "Of course," but refrain from reminding her we won't need it because we are going on a car picnic.

Finally on our way to Peet's Coffee for our latte, we are not on a tight schedule, yet my mother is in a hurry, just as before her accident. That she can't remember where we're going does not seem to affect how fast we need to get there. "Come on. Come on," she says to the first red light we hit. "Thi' i' costing us money. We can't affor' to sit here, goddamni'!"

When we make it through a green light a minute later, she cheers me on. "Oh, good, you ma' it. The man who invented traffi' ligh's was very smar'," she adds.

She is stuck in 1960 when she was a very busy woman with a career, a husband, two teenagers, and an active social life—a person with no time to waste. Also, she has the family frugality gene. Margarine, not butter. Stew, not steak. Used cars and hand-me-down furniture. Sprinklers, not a pool. What part of her frugality isn't wired in, growing up poor goes a long way toward explaining. Whatever the reasons, my mother remains incapable of wasting anything—time, sugar, cereal, even gasoline.

"Where would you like to go for our picnic? "I ask.

"It's u' to you," she says.

"No, really. Lake view, valley view, meadow, oak or redwood trees?" I want *her* to choose.

"It's u' to you," she repeats, so I choose.

We could go to Santa Cruz, an hour away, or Half Moon Bay—a little closer—and eat by the ocean. A nearby nature preserve in the hills where I hike offers a view of the valley. But for our first picnic, I choose a city park not far from where she lives. "Oh, boy," she says when we arrive. "Thi' i' lovely." For her it's always the first time although I have driven her by it many times.

I pull into a parking place where she has a clear view of the grassy field and surrounding oaks and redwoods. She pays more attention to the mommies and preschoolers who walk by on their way to a small playground, a connection to her days as director of a nursery school.

For our lunch, I unpack liverwurst sandwiches with thick slices of red onion, a favorite. I was liberal with mayonnaise on hers. She lost thirty pounds along with her healthy appetite after a surgery a couple years ago and can use the calories. I wrap a paper towel around her sandwich and keep more paper towels and a blue cloth towel handy. It's cool in the shade, so we keep the windows rolled up, and the aroma of raw onion fills the car. Sealed in our snug, oniony cocoon, we savor our meal in silent, shared appreciation.

"Whe's Daddy?" she asks out of the blue.

"He died, Mom. Remember?" I say, wishing I'd left off "re-member."

"Oh," she says, and returns to her sandwich.

Where did she think he's been for the past twenty-five years, I wonder, but realize it takes courage for her even to ask, just as it does for her oft repeated, "Wha' day is i'?" a question she precedes by warning me that she's about to ask something very silly. For all her cognitive limitations, she has some aware-ness of what she's supposed to know.

"Ta' ten dollars ou' of my accou't," she tells me, midway through our picnic. "For foo' and gasoline."

"You paid all my expenses for a very long time. It's my turn," I say.

"Ta' ten dollars ou' of my accou't, plea'," she insists.

"Thank you," I say, but never do. I suspect she realizes this.

At her age and essentially one-handed, it's far too difficult to eat and drink at the same time, so we eat first. The sandwich does have its challenges. "Oh, Kath'een, I di'n' mean to," she cries when drops it on her lap or when a piece of crust or filling falls to the floor. After we finish the eating phase, we can shift to drinking. I pour her portion of the latte into a cup from the set of Louisville stoneware she chose when she married. With her left hand, she lifts the cup ever so carefully from where it sits near the gear shift, most of the time avoiding spills. But the paralysis on her right side causes her to choke on thin liquids. We use all the towels. Always frugal, she stuffs the used paper ones into her Kleenex box. Next time, I plan to collect them before she does.

Though I intend to match her pace, I finish eating long before her. Having left behind a twelve-track life when I retired from teaching, I settle in and enjoy the trees and kids. She urges me to take a walk, but I prefer to sit with her in the car. When she's done, I gather the trash and take it to a nearby garbage can.

"I ha' something for you," she says when I return. "Pu' ou' your han'."

While I was gone, she collected the tiniest bits of refuse from the floor of the car. I take another walk to the garbage can. Recent surgery on her very ripe cataracts make this cleaning

task easy for her. I scheduled the procedure after she insisted
I tell her who was sitting in a chair in our living room and
wouldn't believe me when I told her that the person she saw
was really a coat I'd tossed there. 'Kath'een, you ha' white hair,"
she said to me when the eye surgeon first removed her ban-
dages. I couldn't help laughing.

After lunch, I ask Mom if she'd like to ride along while I run a
few errands. I have in mind the library and a stop at the shopping center. "Do you ha' to shop?" she asks. Even though I
shopped two days before, I say yes. I can't deny her the pleasure
of "helping me" with such a familiar chore.

"Here we are at Safeway," I announce and then go into the
store to buy groceries while Mom helps by waiting.

"Macy's next," I say, unloading the groceries. "I have to return something."

"Oh, goo'," she says, and off we go.

The day has turned warm. I park near an entrance and
once inside, cruise the shoe department before completing my
errand. As I approach the car a half hour later, I notice, to my
amazement, that my mother, visible to anyone passing by, is
sitting there naked from the waist up. Glancing around, I slip
into the driver's seat.

"Mom! What the...! Where the hell is your blouse?" I ask,
fishing it up from between her seat and the console. Out of the
corner my eye, I see a young man approaching. I maneuver her
arms into the garment and pull the two sides over her front.
What was she thinking? Of course, she wasn't. She doesn't.

And asking why she removed her top is both pointless and ridiculous. But I do.

"I wa' hot," she replies.

I have no doubt that's all I'm going to get out of her.

Later, I will share the story with Don. "You know how you're going along in your life, day in, day out, not expecting any big surprises because there haven't been any for a while," I'll say. "And then one day on an outing with your mother, you go back to the car you left her in a few minutes earlier, and she's sitting there in a parking lot, at ninety-something, naked from the waist up, topless, her deflated ninnies exposed for all to see! Because she's hot!"

I make a mental note: on sunny days, park in the shade.

Having more stamina in her nineties than I do in my sixties, Mom would be happy to ride along for hours more when I'm ready to conclude our time together. When she inevitably asks where we're going next, I tell her that we're returning to Pilgrim Haven where she lives. I haven't said "home" since a few years ago after her surgery when I heard her doctor, who was discharging her from the hospital, tell her that she could go home. "I don' know whe' to go," she sobbed, "I don' ha' a home."

Though I have other things to do and places to go, I still hate saying goodbye. I wish I could invite her to live with me. I can't give up wanting to be the daughter who could. Mostly, I wish I could give her the life she deserves. Yet along with these thoughts and feelings runs relief that soon I'll return to the rest of my life.

"I nee' he'p," she reminds me, as I begin the transfer from the car to her wheelchair. "Ho' me, ho' me, ho' me," she says as I lift her into it. I am not fast enough to gather everything before she begins asking for her Kleenex box, day pack, footrest....

"I don' know whe' I live," she says anxiously.

"Right there," I say, indicating the white wooden building with pink shutters. "See the driveway?" I ask, pointing to the asphalt.

"No," she says.

"Where the white posts are?"

"No," she says, more agitated.

"We're going to go down that driveway and turn right onto the pink sidewalk, then go through the door at the end of the sidewalk."

"I don' see," she tells me.

Her concerns escalate once we're inside. "Whe' will I go?" she asks, in panic.

"I can take you to your room, or we can see what's going on in the lounge," I say.

"Ye', but whe' will I go," she asks again, beginning to cry. "You don' understan'."

She's right. I've done everything I can think of to ease her anxiety—but not what she needs or wants or expects—which I can't even begin to guess. Then: wait a minute, I tell myself, I *am* doing all the right things. *She's* the one who doesn't understand. I just want this to be over. I take a breath and remind myself the picnic was a success. She loved it. Next week, we'll try the coast.

Seven years and thousands of picnics later, nothing about them has changed. The contents of our sandwiches don't vary much other than Mom's being pureed—wheat bread and fillings like tuna, egg, minced turkey, or soft cheese and the occasional liverwurst with onion.

With the missing blouse incident in mind, I park in the shade on hot days. Each time I leave her in the car, I tell her how long I'll be. She always responds, "Ta' all the ti' you wan'." Before shutting the driver's side door, I lean back into the car. "And keep your shirt on," I say. She looks at me with a puzzled expression. "Remember when you took off your shirt in the Macy's parking lot?" By this time, I am laughing.

She smiles to be polite and says, "Oh, ye'."

Sometimes though, she'll get the joke. Sometimes she'll come back with a snappy "You wish." For the most part, we amuse each other by drawing heavily on our repertoire of one-liners, amassed over a lifetime of storytelling and kidding. What was funny once makes us laugh again in the repeating.

For a while, I looked for a parking spot where my mother could watch people while I did errands. Then she mentioned how much she also enjoyed watching cars pass. I realized that I could *never* fail to please her in any of my choices, whether a type of parking place, a sandwich, or a destination for an outing. She thanks me for every little thing I do. The joy that comes of pleasing her so easily is among her greatest gifts to me. "No one will ever love you as much as your mother," my father always told me. It took me a while to really understand what he meant.

As to the returns to the nursing home after our forays, the ones that end in tears are far outweighed by the good versions when she recognizes her building, when the trip from the car to the Health Center goes smoothly, when I can leave her just inside the door rather than take her all the way to her room or to the activity room. "Go ho' to the childre'," she'll say on a good day, turning her wheelchair to face down the hallway before I even say goodbye. "I'll go by myse'f," she tells me.

The ritual of the easy leave-taking continues. "Be good," I tell her.

"Tha's impossib'," she retorts.

We joke briefly about whether she knows where she is going—she always claims she doesn't—or whether she can get there under her own steam. That's harder these days, but my mother is nothing if not determined.

I can never be certain of seeing her again. I want the last thing she hears me say to be "I love you" and save these most important words for when she's underway, hunched over in her chair, using her good leg to push off the floor, gaining a couple of inches at a time.

I don't remember telling her I loved her during my growing up years. I don't remember telling her during my young adult life either, but it's been important for a long time now to speak the words. Since she's almost deaf, I have to shout then follow her back down the hall if she doesn't indicate that she's heard.

"I love you, Mom."

Sometimes she replies that she loves me too. Sometimes, she just shrugs. I like hearing the words and wish she would speak them but recognize that a shrug is more her style. It says that she's fully engaged in her efforts to get back to her room and can't be bothered with something that so obviously goes without saying.

Chapter 20
I Want My Money Back!

On Thursdays, my husband Don takes my mother along on his errands. When I mention how much I appreciate this gesture, he says, "I like your mother." Everyone does.

At her insistence, their routine recently evolved to include stops at a driving range where she used to spend countless hours watching my father hit balls. The two men— both tall, blue-eyed, and kind—have become indistinguishable in her mind, which led to her urging Don, who has played the game but is not a golfer, to hit balls.

Going to the driving range is predictable and familiar, the neural pathways underlying it worn as deep as the ruts in the Oregon Trail. Watching Don hit balls, as she once watched my father, puts her topsy-turvy world right again. When she's with him at the driving range (I accompanied them once), the expression on her face is like that of someone who after being lost for a very long time, suddenly recognizes where she is. In my mother's case, a string of memories has returned that permit her a rare sense of continuity. "Good, good," she says when the balls travel straight and far then nods encouragingly when they don't.

My husband also takes my mother to lunch. He used to buy her a hot dog on their trips to Costco, but once when he left her in the cafe to finish eating while he shopped, she choked. He was in line when he heard a store employee calling his name, first and last. I've won something, he thought. Then he glanced toward the café and noticed a dozen paramedics surrounding my mother. The Costco employee who gave her the Heimlich maneuver told my husband that she had gagged and turned blue. Someone called 9-1-1.

Miraculously, my mother managed to give the store employee my husband's first and last name for the page. My husband and I still marvel at her coming up with his last name—in total, she knows six people by their first names—but it's her remarks at the ER that drew laughter from those of us who know her well.

During the six hours we spent at the ER waiting for a doctor to examine my mother, she asked over and over where she was and why. Over and over, I explained she was in the hospital, that she'd choked on a hot dog and that someone had helped her spit it out. Now, she was being checked for broken ribs. "Wher' my ho' dog?" she wanted to know.

"Long gone and good riddance," I said countless times.

"Well, I wan' my ho' dog back," she said.

"It's in the garbage now." "

"Then I wan' my money back," she said.

She still answers hot dogs whenever I ask what she would like for dinner—code for let's have something cheap and easy.

"How about meatloaf?" I say. "No more hot dogs. Remember what happened at Costco?"

She doesn't, so I repeat the story. "Oh," she says. "Kath'een, I ha' a ve'y poo' memory."

I pureed a hot dog for her once, but she insisted it wasn't a hot dog, so I gave up on that idea and over time, on serving most of her other favorite foods too, at least in solid form.

Chapter 21
Raw Onions and Rocky Road

As a little kid, I picked at the standard American fare my mother prepared—meals of the brown, white, and green sort. But once during a family vacation in Carmel the year I turned twelve, Mom suggested we try a Mexican restaurant.

"Eww," I said.

"Don't look at me," said my brother.

"I was looking forward to a burger and shake, Dorothy," my father said.

My father, brother, and I—less adventurous eaters—headed toward the burger joint. Mom set off alone toward the Mexican restaurant. I had barely slid into the booth when I began to feel so sorry for her, I couldn't let her eat alone.

I had noticed the attractive restaurant on our strolls around town—a converted adobe house set back from the street with succulent gardens on either side of a brick pathway that led to the blue door. Colored lights and bright paper garlands decorated the windows.

I spotted my mother at a table by one of them. I didn't need a menu, and she didn't offer one. I had no expectation of liking any of the food. I liked mashed potatoes and bread and pasta, white foods without much taste.

"Try a cheese enchilada," she said, when I sat down opposite her. "The man at the next table is having one."

"That lumpy gooey thing with all that red sauce?" I whispered, glancing at the dish she'd indicated.

"Just try it," she said.

The sauce was creamy and mild like Campbell's tomato soup lightly spiced, and the tortilla and melted cheese tasted a little like a grilled cheese sandwich. After three thoughtful bites and swallows, I looked at Mom. "I like it," I said in surprise.

Including that enchilada dinner, I figure Mom and I have since eaten more than twenty thousand meals together. I once did the math. Never fond of cooking, she has always relished eating, and I like to think the meals I prepare for her outshine the institutional food where she now lives even if she does claim she can't taste anything. This doesn't seem to dull her appetite or enthusiasm for eating or mine for preparing foods I know she once liked. "Oh, boy, liver and onions," she'll say.

"Good sandwi'," she said once, midway through a liverwurst sandwich at a Tuesday picnic.

"Can you really taste it?" I asked her.

"No," she said.

"Then how do you know it's good?" I asked.

"I'd know i' it was bad," she said laughing.

On Sunday nights when Mom comes for dinner, the first words out of her mouth are, "Ca' I he'p?" Her wheelchair doesn't fit in the kitchen—where the tasks are too difficult anyway—so I give her laundry to fold at the table, small items like napkins, hand towels, and underwear. When there's no clean laundry to fold, I'll unfold a few things and deliver them to her. She sets about this way of helping me with pleasure.

After she finishes the laundry, no matter what the season, she says, "The bes' thin' abou' thi' hou' is the firep'ace." In cool weather when we have a fire, she rolls close to the hearth, folds her hands in her lap, sinks deeper into her wheelchair, and closes her eyes. I've concluded that the light and warmth of the fire activate intact pleasure pathways deep in her brain.

When dinner's ready, I roll her to her place at the head of the table. "No potato," she says every time I set a plate in front of her. She never asks if I'm serving potatoes. Often I am not. She just repeats in a panicky voice. "No potato, I'm slimmin'."

"You don't need to watch your weight anymore" I say.

"I'm slimmin'," she says.

"That was the old days, Mom, when you and Barbara were always on a diet. You're already slim now."

"No potato," she repeats.

Just another way she is stuck in 1960. And another way I am stuck saying things I know she either doesn't comprehend or are, as far as she's concerned, beside the point.

Back when Mom was in her early nineties and had moved to skilled nursing, she could still eat just about anything—that is her teeth had not yet fallen out. She loved salads, spareribs, raw onions, anything Chinese or Mexican, and rocky road ice

cream. As she lost teeth and as swallowing became more difficult, the nursing home switched her to a soft food diet and
then pureed. At my house, I continued to mince her lasagna or
burger or quesadilla or creamed onions and offer her favorite
soft foods like avocados and crab. I also found a type of bread
she could eat on our picnics. My blended version of a liver-
wurst-red onion-avocado sandwich is not a bad substitute for
the real thing. She liked my blended BLTs also, although they
were runny. But finally, I had to switch to pureed foods too at
our Sunday dinners. I once used my Cuisinart to process an
entire take-out Chinese meal—course by course—from won-
ton soup to Mongolian lamb, dry braised green beans, and rice.
Nowadays, I also use a product from the pharmacy to thicken
her drinks, her bourbon and water and her coffee. Whether
it's liquids thickened to honey consistency or solids thinned
to pudding texture, all Mom's foods require processing so she
won't choke or inhale them. Even so, as she approaches ninety-
eight, most meals are two-towel affairs, with multiple chok-
ing episodes, the occasional sneeze, and at times, mysterious
moaning. We don't go to restaurants anymore.

These days, each bite of a meal is a tiny miracle. Feeding
herself since the accident was always hit or miss—she lacked
muscle control, and her movements were jerky—and it's even
harder now that she's old. Yet Mom methodically gathers
each bite and lifts it haltingly above her plate, pauses, opens
her mouth, then tilting her head toward the utensil, brings the
spoon quickly to her lips. She retrieves inevitable bits and blobs
from her bib and lap as soon as they fall. Our old dog Tessa has

happily settled next to her through fourteen years of Sunday dinners, holiday, and family celebrations, cleaning up spills that made it to the floor, most unintentional and I suspect, some on purpose.

Although eating requires immense concentration, not once in all the meals we've eaten together has Mom expressed frustration or become angry, or complained or apologized, unless she tipped over a glass. "I di'n' mean to, I di'n' mean to," she'll repeat if she spills a drink. She finishes her meal, says it's delicious, and thanks me many times over. "Won'erfu', won'erfu'. Good dinner, Kath'een." Or "Than' you for brea'fast. Let's go out for lun'."

"That was dinner we just had," I might remind her.

"Oh," she'll say. "Very good brea'fast."

I could serve her pureed canned spaghetti, and she would say wonderful and delicious. But I'll keep offering her old favorites. Making a meal is a small thing compared to her pleasure. Similar to how helping me with the laundry must make *Mom* feel good, the truth is cooking for her makes *me* feel good. And it's dawning on me that quite possibly, she has always known this.

Nowadays, I help my mother with the last few bites after she has carefully scraped them into mounds. Only this year has she reverted to eating with a spoon instead of a fork, and not until a few weeks ago, did she expect me to feed her part of her meal.

Awkward as she is, a trace of how she once moved is still visible—in the way she grips a spoon with her thumb and first two fingers, ring and little fingers curled under them, and in flashes as she scoops food onto her spoon. There's a certain elegance in the way she picks up a glass, plastic these days because real glass is too heavy. Little finger in the air, she sips in queen-like fashion, albeit noisily. From my place at the table next to her, I capture freeze-frame mental snapshots and create the ghostly presence of my young mother. I assemble clues unnoticeable to anyone but me, extrapolate from split seconds of familiar gestures, and string them together in my imagination to see her as she once was.

I try not to dwell on the dwindling number of meals we'll have together. I resist imagining the future. She started off so far into it. How much more limited can she become?

Chapter 22
All in the Family

"Whe's Don?" my mother asks, after a recent Sunday dinner.

Behind her right shoulder and across the room, the TV screen glows. My husband has retired to the living room, his bare foot just visible from where I'm sitting. She can't hear the creaks and clunks of his recliner or the game on TV either. "Watching basketball," I shout.

She nods. "Typical," she says.

Having been a sports widow all her married days, Mom never really holds the hours Don watches sports against him. As fond of him as he is of her, she occasionally acts as if I don't deserve him.

When she moved to assisted living, I had bought her a phone with large push buttons and taught her to use it. One night, she called me. "I orde'd a roll-awa' bed for you, so you can come and li' wi' me now."

"Why would I do that?" I asked.

"The divor'," she said.

"But there's no divorce," I said, annoyed at her for thinking my husband would want one.

"Send the roll-away bed back."

"Kath'een, are you sure?"

"I should know," I said.

I could tell by her tone of voice she was not convinced. Now, at every one of our outings, we have a similar irritating exchange about where Don is. "At work," used to satisfy her. Then he retired. For the first few years after, I explained that he no longer went to work. "Retired," I said. But she always gave me a worried look. So I've taken to telling her he's at the store or visiting one of our kids.

"You hope," she replies every time.

Maybe she's expressing her own deeply buried fears from long ago, or hers for me. For an instant before attributing her comments to crossed wires, I wonder if she sees something I don't.

"Don is very ni' to me," Mom says over and over.

"He likes you," I say.

Don had agreed without hesitation to have Mom live with us when her home care arrangements fell apart so spectacularly in 1987, the car she was in sailing backwards off a cliff. I don't recall what he said four years later when I finally moved her to assisted living, but my daughters weighed in with the natural candor of children.

Laura, age nine, said, "I'm glad and I'm sad Grandma's gone. I'm glad because it's better without her. I'm sad because it's kind of empty around here."

Six-year-old Sarah said, "I'm glad. She was almost everywhere blocking the way. We get to be with you more. She was always calling, 'Kath'een, Kath'een.' And I don't miss the crying."

Sarah wasn't referring to her grandmother's tears of frustration when someone didn't immediately do what she asked. Sarah meant the hardest of the hard times when Mom took to her bed for the day and cried the tears any mother would, who was totally dependent on her daughter. "I don' wan' to be a bu'den," she would say.

"You are not a burden. I want you with me," I told her.

She was inconsolable at those times, but fortunately, they were rare.

When Sarah was eleven, she wrote a story about her grandmother. "It doesn't take much to make her happy. She generally is happy when she sees my mom and/or me and/or my sister. It's sort of sad that my grandma is losing her memory, but she's not sad or angry or disappointed, so why should I be? I'm just happy she's alive and healthy. I love my grandma."

Sarah went on to write that her grandma was very concerned about our health and called at least six times a day to check on us. Laura once acted out one of these phone exchanges.

"Hi, Kath'een."

"Hi, Grandma, It's Laura.

"Oh, hi Sarah. Is Kath'een ho'?"

"It's Laura, Grandma. Mom's not home."

"Te' her I ca'd, p'ease."

"OK, Grandma."

"Than' you, Kath'een."

Even though my mother often mixes up their names, she knows my girls best of all the members of our expanding family. There are others she recognizes: my stepchildren Sam, Michael, and Jennifer and Laura's life partner Mia and her sister Aaliyah. Mike moved to San Diego and started a yacht outfitting business. Mom pretends to recognize the members of his large family, who live too far away to visit often: wife Francine and before her, his ex-wife Pam, and his seven kids: Vanessa, Melissa, Teresa, Nick, Anna, Molly, and Jesse.

Now thirty-one and twenty-eight, Laura is a nurse, and Sarah works with old people at an assisted living facility. The girls still play Crazy Eights with their grandmother, visit her at the nursing home, and laugh with her—and yes, sometimes, at her.

Back during their teenage and early adult years whenever the girls were having a hard time, I counted on my mother— especially if there was a hint of self-pity.

"Let's go see Grandma," I'd say.

"Oh, Sarah," Mom would say, lighting up, or, "Oh, Laura," randomly. "I'm so gla' you' here."

"Hi, Grandma," they'd say, in a flat tone.

"How a' you?"

"OK," they'd say, withholding their story about the friend who didn't invite them to a birthday party or the disappointing grade on an assignment.

"Are we goin' ou'?" my mother would ask, her eyes bright with anticipation.

"Where would you like to go, Mom?" I'd ask.

"Oh, Rome," she'd say.

The girls would smile.

"An' dancin'," Mom would add. "I wa' to go dancin'."

Bigger smiles.

Bu' wait," she'd say. "Firs', I ha' somethi' for you."

Then she'd slip them a treasure from the top drawer of her bedside table where she kept pilfered items.

"Hurry. Hi' it," she'd say, as if she had passed them a stolen diamond necklace instead of a package of crushed Saltines or yet another stuffed animal won at bingo.

Soon, we'd all be laughing, troubles forgotten.

Every time I drive away from the nursing home, a mix of relief and gratitude tinged with guilt passes over me. I can leave the responsibility of caring for my mother to others and resume my life. Yet with Mom now in her late nineties, I still wonder about having her live with me again. Despite memories of overwhelming responsibilities that put me on tranquilizers, there's a part of me that says a good daughter would care for her aging mother. After all, in the Philippines or India, she'd be living with family.

When I mention having her return to spend the last years of her life with us, Don doesn't object and leaves the decision to me. Whatever else he thinks remains unstated. So far, I have not acted on my urge. Her needs are daunting, and she thrives on an assortment of other people and activities her care home provides. Sadly too, I realize that overwhelmed wouldn't approach describing my state if she lived with us again. It might even send Don looking for a roll-away bed somewhere. But then again, probably not.

Part 5

"I am dumb. I can't remembe' anythin'. I can't do anythin', but I'm smar' enou' to know I'm lucky."

Dorothy Canrinus

Chapter 23
Present Moments Only

"I'm in love," my ninety-seven-year-old mother tells me softly.

The family is gathered in the living room after Sunday dinner to watch the closing ceremony of the Olympics—Laura and her partner Mia, my husband, mother, and I. Most of the time in conversation, my mother repeats the same three-or-four-word phrases and a few single words like "good," "wonderful," or "fine." The raciest thing Mom ever said was at the dinner table once, when her blouse rode up to expose her naked breast. "Dorothy, your stomach's showing," Don said, and pulled her blouse down.

"Tha's not my stomach," she shot back, flashing him a look.

But confiding that she's in love? I do a double take and ask his name, although I don't expect her to be able to tell me. She looks down at her lap, murmurs she doesn't know, then looks up and spots my husband across the room.

"I'm in lo' wi' your husban'," she says.

Since the exchanges between my mother and me are mostly contextual and scripted, when she deviates from fifty-year-old patterns, my thoughts go immediately to the possibility that she might be getting better or possibly be more cognitively intact than I give credit and overlook experiences like when I drove her to see the "tin box" after a picnic on the Santa Cruz wharf. She had lived there for seventeen years, fifteen with my father. Trees and bushes had grown so much in the twenty years since she moved, even I was momentarily disoriented.

"Do you know where we are?" I asked Mom.

"Whe'?" she said.

"At DeAnza Mobile Home Park," I said. "2395 Delaware Street."

She didn't say anything. I slowed the car.

"There's the clubhouse where Dad played pool, and you two went to potlucks."

Still no response.

I wound past the clubhouse and down the street toward the sharp left turn to her place, past new units with wood siding that gave them the look of real houses, past old ones now partially obscured by lush landscaping. We passed unfamiliar residents walking unfamiliar dogs.

"There's where you lived—Space 192," I said. "At the end, on the right."

"I don' remembe' a thing," she said, looking the opposite direction from where I was pointing.

We never went back.

Yet recently, my husband reported that when he took her on an errand to San Francisco, she said, "Nice day. No fog," as the tall buildings downtown came into view, just as anyone might. But my mother usually stops at "Nice day." "No fog," indicates she recognized the City and recalled typical weather there.

Then after a lunch in my backyard with The Friends, she rolled her wheelchair over to the gate and tried to get out into the driveway. "Where are you going?" I asked.

"To fee' the dog," she said.

"Let's feed the dog later," I suggested.

"But he's hungry now," she said.

"How about if I feed him?" I said. "Then we'll play cards." She nodded. I suspect she'd tripped onto an old memory link, which one was unclear. Was she going to feed my dog who'd been dead for three years or her dog gone forty years, or maybe one of the family dogs from my childhood sixty years back? Could this tripping indicate regeneration, synaptic reconnections?

I decided to call a neuro-rehab facility to ask about their program. But when the person on the phone asked the date of Mom's injury, and I told her 1960, she fell silent. Too much time had passed. Evidence of change didn't qualify my mother for therapy.

"When did you realize she would not get better?" people ask. I have to admit that I haven't yet. She won't walk again or speak clearly or have a short-term memory, but maybe as her brain shrinks with age, scar tissue will shift and neurons will transmit again, as in, "No fog." A few old memories might return. This might be fantasy. Any gains would be offset by losses due to aging, and in any case, they do not explain the "I'm in love" comment.

My mother did make people laugh. She was the life of the party and a little on the outrageous side. Was her intention even now to entertain? "Why did you say you were in love?" I ask her, unable to stifle the question.

"I ha' a very poo' memo'y," she reminds me, and retreats behind closed eyes. She's already forgotten her remark. Folding her hands, she hunches deeper into her wheelchair, a half-smile playing about her lips.

Chapter 24
The Deal

"Very goo'," Mom says, after I help her with the last spoonful of another Sunday meal—pureed Spicy Moroccan Chicken. As I reach over to tuck a stray strand of hair under her headband, my fingers brush against the soft skin at her temple. She pulls back the way I once did when she fussed with my hair.

She sets her spoon and plastic glass at the center of her plate, a signal for me to clear. I do so and replace her soiled bib with a clean one, noting that the purple vest she's wearing belongs to another nursing home resident. In her right mind, she wouldn't have been caught dead in purple, but it's been some time since she was in her right mind.

Except for two deep wrinkles that start on either side of her nose and disappear under her chin, her face is relatively unlined for a person approaching her hundredth birthday. I sit down again and stare at her. I want to preserve everything about her in memory: her toothless smile, the knotted joints in her fingers, the smooth skin on the backs of her hands, even her garbled voice. I don't want to lose her.

As if sensing that I am studying her, Mom looks up, a trace of hope in her alert gaze. She moves her coffee cup aside. Most

Sunday nights we play cards after dinner, but as eager as Mom is to play, she won't come right out and suggest a game. She never demands or pressures me. She leaves whether we play entirely up to me.

I do not love these games. Often, they are like climbing Mount Everest, one more chore on Sunday night. But when I make excuses not to play at all or skip a second game, the corners of her mouth dip down. Fortunately, I know she doesn't love me for the person I think I should be, the one who would always play no matter what.

When I turn to open the drawer and get out the cards, and Mom's eyes light up, nothing but her joy matters a whit. Palpable and contagious, it instantly melts any lingering notions of what I might be doing instead. We sit, my mother at the head of my kitchen table and I around the corner—these days close enough to peek at her hand—and we play—two white-haired old ladies.

While dealing out the cards for our game, I ask if she remembers teaching me Russian Bank. "I remembe' p'aying," she says, "no' teachi,'."

I can't suppress a brief wish that she remembered the day that was so special to me, but decide not to explore the thought that there was no special significance to that afternoon for her.

In the manner of a surgical nurse, I place the cards firmly between the thumb and fingers of her good left hand, six cards, not the standard eight, which would be too many for her grip. Fingers that once clasped a brush to untangle knots from my permed hair are now twisted and bent with age. Their tips no longer line up with her knuckles but veer off at unexpected angles. When she tries to fan her cards, they fall on the table, on her lap, on the floor. "I'm so'y. I'm so'y. I di'n' mean to," she says, swiping at the saliva at the corner of her mouth as she speaks. I hand her cards back to her swabbing them and her with the towel I keep handy.

Now that she's lost her hearing and even more of her memory, our games are fully choreographed: our spots at the table, the tap on the deck that indicates time to draw, my prompts to remind her of the rules down to the inflection in my voice, even the nods and gestures to signal it's the other's turn or that we've played our last card. I make sure that most of the time, she wins.

Sometime in the past year, she lost the ability to play without help. Since she might never win without it—and she loves to win—I've become adept at cheating. Mine is a different kind of cheating from when my brother and I caught her slipping part of her hand into a drawer to avoid losing and having to do the dishes. I glance discretely at her hand and lay down a card in a suit she has. Or sneak a wild eight onto the draw pile for her. I'll draw when I don't have to. We haven't played cribbage for years. Too complicated. And nowadays, even with reminders, she'll randomly switch from Crazy Eights to Solitaire mid-game, yet whenever I get out the cards again after dinner, she can't hide her delight.

One night while pots simmer, and a roast chicken rests on the counter—Cuisinart nearby—I gather the cards to deal a before-dinner game. This particular Sunday, deep in slogging up Everest mode, I can't help thinking about the other things I need to be doing. But Don has already played two games and retreated to the living room to watch the news. And the girls are off living their big lives, so I can't ask them to take over while I pack for an upcoming visit to family in Portland, or prepare for the small group book discussion a teacher friend asked me to lead tomorrow morning, or memorize a section of the new Finnish song for chorus.

Instead, here I am about to play another game of Crazy Eights that she won't remember playing within minutes after we finish. Nonetheless, I force myself to continue. I can't deny her one of the high points of her week, the other being bingo at the facility.

"Will you cheat?" I ask before we begin.

"Of cour'," she replies.

"Feeling lucky?" I ask.

"Alway'," she says. "I ha' to."

I wonder what she means by "have to." But instead of asking, I say, "You like to win."

"I li' to p'ay," she says.

Her eyes shine with pleasure. She gathers her hand. I help her fan it.

She squints—brow wrinkled in concentration. She's playing to win but losing won't faze her. "I don't have a single card to play," I inform her. "You go first."

She tries not to laugh but can't help herself. "D'aw," she says.

I draw and draw again. She laughs.

"Mom, it's not very nice of you to laugh at my lousy cards."
I draw another card, frown, and tuck it in my hand, all the
while savoring every one of her guffaws.

"D'aw, Kath'een," she says again, laughing harder.

Our game lasts longer than most, but finally, Mom flashes
me her grin. "I'm ou'.

Well played," I say to her.

"I ha'a goo' teacher," she says, though it was she who taught
me.

"Well played," I repeat to myself, as I put away the cards.

There are few things in life I like better than losing to my
mother. Tedious as the games are, I am committed to playing them until she no longer can. And for the same reason she
taught them to me in the first place, for love.

Before returning to the kitchen to finish making dinner, a
question pops into my head. I don't expect Mom to be able to
answer but can't resist asking anyway.

"And what do you have to say about your life?" I ask.

"Tha' e'ryon' shou' be as lucky as I am," she replies, without
hesitation.

I'm shocked. "Lucky!" I say. "How so?"

In contrast to her usual two or three-word response, she
answers in complete sentences.

"I ha' you, an' I ha' Don, an' Laura an' Sarah," she says.

That's not enough, I think. How can she not wish for anything to have been different?

"I am dumb. I can't remembe' anythin'. I can't do anythin',"
she continues. "But I'm smar' enou' to know I'm lucky."

She pauses and then adds, "An' you're lucky too," looking at me as if I'd be in total agreement.

How could she possibly think we'd been lucky when in so many ways, we had both been so unlucky? What could she mean? I don't feel lucky. Lucky would be if she'd remained my mother, instead of becoming my child.

Mom must have noticed how shocked I am. "Deal, Kath'een," she says, effectively cutting me off from slipping further into self-pity. "Jus' p'ay."

Chapter 25
The Lady with the Crown

Thanks to caller ID, if the phone rings, I know what to expect. When it's skilled nursing, muscles tense. Wondering if this is The Call, I pick up.

"This is the nurse caring for your mother tonight," the voice begins. "I'm calling to let you know she fell out of bed again."

"Is she OK?"

"Oh, yes, but I'm required to report to you."

"Thank you. Tell her I love her, and I'll be by in the morning."

I've answered the same way to all manner of reports. Your mother cut her hand, or she's bleeding, or she bumped her leg, or fell out of her chair. There was even a call from the director of nursing to say, "Your mother kicked an aide and sent her to the hospital."

"Really?" I had to ask. "At ninety-four and partially paralyzed?" After which, I did nothing.

But once a duty nurse called to tell me my mother had been crying for hours, and no one could figure out what was wrong. I drove over.

"Who" takin' care of Gram?" she asked, when I arrived at her bedside.

"Oh, Mom, she died a long time ago." I didn't mention that sixty years had passed since Gram's death. The number would have made no sense to her.

"I remember liking to spend time with her," I told my mother. "As soon as you let me out the door in the morning, I ran to her house. She'd be getting dressed on the furnace register in her living room. I remember her funny skin-colored undershirts and print dresses with buttons and belts."

My mother's eyes closed, but I continued. "She was old and wrinkled and pinned her white hair up on top of her head. I wondered what she looked like without anything on, but I never got to her house early enough to find out."

My mother smiled. "I remember she fed me milk toast in a highchair in her kitchen," I went on. "She taught me my prayers in Piemontese before you taught them to me in English. And she never scolded me, even for sneaking the candies I discovered in her top dresser drawer."

"She li'd chi'dren," Mom said, and drifted off to sleep.

Among other alerts that required action, there was, "Your mother is having trouble breathing," or "Your mother is vomiting blood." One resulted in removal of part of her intestine, a procedure discouraged by every medical person I talked with in the ER. "She's demented," they said, incredulous that I would consider surgery to save her life. "She'll need skilled nursing care."

"She's been demented for over fifty years, and she lives in skilled nursing. You examined her. You must have noticed that all she wants is to get out of here because her bingo game's at 3."

"She won't survive the anesthetic," the anesthesiologist told me as he readied her for surgery.

I told him he didn't know my mother. "First of all, she made it to 92."

"Yes, this is something in her favor," he said.

"And secondly, she has a remarkable spirit," I continued.

I could almost see his eyes roll. As he swung the gurney toward the operating room, she threw her arm in the air and called out, "Lunch is on me." The doc cracked a smile.

After surgery, she was put on a respirator. I sat by her bed during the day and told her the story of her life, starting over when I reached her current hospitalization. Her oxygen numbers were still low a week after surgery, so I gave permission for removal of the breathing device. Contrary to what was expected, her numbers bounced back to normal. Before the transfer from Intensive Care to a medical floor, she insisted I put her shoes at the foot of her bed where she could see them, then asked for her purse, took out a comb and ran it through her hair. Though full recovery took a while, she's seven years out from that surgery and still enjoying life.

Best of all was something that happened the year my mother wore her cardboard birthday crown every day—low on her forehead so it wouldn't fall off. I was surprised when I showed up for our picnic to find her sporting it. It resembled something from a fast-food kiddie meal. She wore it to Sunday dinner the week after her birthday party, and the staff at Pilgrim Haven intimated that she almost never took it off. After a month of seeing it, I hardly noticed. The mothers at the park where we picnicked would smile at us, and I'd think, how nice, before I remembered the crown. Similar smiles would appear on the faces of other patients at the doctor's office and on passersby in the parking lots at the grocery store and library. At Costco, Don reported my mother nodded when smiling strangers asked if it was her birthday.

One Sunday night when I dropped off after dinner, a nursing assistant took me aside to tell me about a little boy who'd come to visit his great-grandmother and lost the teddy bear he took everywhere. "We looked and looked for the animal," she said, "in the resident's room, in the lounge, and on the patio. We couldn't find it anywhere. So we searched everywhere again and still no luck. Finally, we asked the boy himself when he last saw it. 'The lady with the crown had it'," he said.

Chapter 26
A Trip Back in Time

My mother doesn't remember the months following her accident or much else since, and her long-term memory of life before that is limited. My father and brother are gone. Mom and I are all that's left, two wrinkled, gnarly-knuckled old ladies.

For the last half century, I've wanted to forget those agonizing first days and weeks and months after the accident. But when a news article mentions the possible sale of O'Connor Hospital, something compels me to go there one last time.

Nothing about the approach to the hospital is familiar--not the office buildings on O'Connor Drive or the roar of traffic from a nearby freeway, not the concrete planters with their clusters of coral geraniums. Nothing reminds me of those long-ago trips to the hospital where my mother lay in a coma.

"She's still asleep," my father would tell us, reporting on his morning visits at dinner. "She's still asleep," he'd say when he returned home from his nightly visits.

After weeks of waiting anxiously at home, my brother and I took to accompanying him, hoping each time that we too would finally be allowed to see our mother. She had a cerebral hemorrhage, our father had explained. Her brain bled and swelled and deprived her brain cells of oxygen. That she had a diagnosis meant nothing to me. She was unconscious. All I cared about was whether she would come back to us and be our mother again.

Since those months when we waited for her to wake up, I avoided driving anywhere near O'Connor, and when that wasn't possible, I averted my eyes. I wanted to forget. And now the dreaded place, so solid and unchanging, like my life before the time I spent there, was itself facing a major transition.

As I approach the five-story beige building, my chest tightens. My breathing quickens to a pant and slows again. There is a tingling pressure behind my eyes. These sensations, I recognize.

Outside the main entrance to the hospital stands a marble statue of the Virgin Mary. Her pose is familiar, eyes closed, face serene. But she is small and grey, not large and white as in memory. She holds out small arms, hands open, palms up. Where people have touched her for a blessing, the stone is polished to a high sheen. A card propped at her feet reads, "Blessed Mary, thank you for hearing our prayers." Whoever wrote that must be among the few very lucky ones. If only…

Hurrying into the lobby, I scan the room for the other statue of Mary, the one I remember, but only find one of St. Vincent de Paul. Inside too, where my brother and I waited for our mother to return to us so our lives could resume, nothing is familiar—not the linoleum or the gift shop, not the spindly Ficus trees, or the chrome chairs. What did I expect after fifty-some years?

Dismayed that nothing takes me back, I sit down on one of the chairs and wonder what I am doing there. Suppressing the urge to leave in spite of my disappointment, I just watch. A man in a lab coat and turban steps in. A nurse in violet scrubs pushes a wheelchair with a woman holding a baby toward the main entrance. A man wearing a camouflage hoody and red running shoes follows them carrying a car seat with a pink liner. Under the figure of the crucified Christ on a wall across the room, two women tap on their phones.

I sit and wait. Still, nothing sharpens the few fragmented memories from after my mother's accident. Yet I'm not ready to leave. I want to remember. I close my eyes. I breathe in deeply the hospital smell. Exhale then inhale. Again and again until the present does indeed give way to the past. Day becomes night. And I remember how in the darkness, table lamps glowed warm and golden, their soft light reflected on the polished stone floor. The large-leafed plants in ceramic pots unfurled upward, the room silent and empty.

In it, a tall thin teenage girl and a slightly younger boy sat at opposite ends of a long couch. Next to the girl a white marble statue of Mary rose heavenward from her pedestal. The girl chewed the nails on one hand and gripped the armrest with the other. She stared at the stone Mother of God, searching for the slightest movement in her cold fingers, a sign that the girl's pleas had been heard.

After a while, she began to pace between the couch and the front windows. She made her way toward the doorway to the first-floor rooms, then circled the lobby to calm herself. Click-tap.

Click-tap. Her heels struck the hard surface of the floor, the clipped purposeful sound a dramatic contrast to the churning emotions inside her.

Her course brought her back to the couch where the boy slipped farther into his slouch, his eyes half-closed. He worked his hands deeper into his pockets. A nursing nun passed without looking at the children, her white winged headpiece like a clipper ship under sail. The girl heard the whoosh of the nun's long dark-blue habit, the soft ticking of the wooden rosary beads that hung from her waist. The girl opened her mouth to scream at the retreating figure. "Help me! Help! Help! Tell God I want my mother back. I beg you. I'll do anything. Please." But no sound escaped.

Two nurses in starched white uniforms and caps leaned their heads together just outside the double-doors to the first-floor rooms. The girl slid to the edge of the couch, expectant. She was certain the worst had happened. But when her father returned, he repeated the same words he had said for weeks. "She's still asleep."

For a moment, the relief of knowing her mother was alive displaced the fear her mother would never wake up. She grabbed a breath and sank back into the abyss of loss.

I open my eyes to bright sunlight. Nearby, a woman leans over a little boy seated next to her. His legs are too short to reach the floor.

"Stay right here. Everything's going to be all right," she tells him. "I'll be back," she says "You'll be OK."

He nods several times, not in agreement but to indicate he heard. His mother disappears. His eyes are red. He doesn't smile or look around. He shoves his hands deep into his pockets.

Please, I say to myself. Let him be OK. Let everything be all right. If I had the power, I'd will it to be so. If I still believed, I'd drop to my knees and pray.

When I leave the hospital and walk to my car, the ache of longing accompanies me. "You again," I say, and jam the gearstick into drive.

Chapter 27
The Cards You're Dealt

Until some forty years after the accident, I told myself that neurological damage protected my mother from knowing how different she was. The alternative was too painful. Then Mom's best friend Barbara told me a story that forced me to change my view.

Shortly before my mother was discharged from O'Connor, Barbara took her a framed photo of a luau from that long-gone world of health and normalcy. In the photo, Mom, Barbara and Louie, a friend who owned the local Shell station, stand laughing, arm-in-arm. He has on a turquoise Hawaiian shirt, and the women are wearing muumuus, my mother with a red bandana tied around her hips, a yellow lei, and a woven palm hat. Barbara handed her the photo. My mother gave it a single glance then pitched it across the room where it shattered against the wall. She knew how much she had lost.

Yet she rarely mentions now being unable to fix a meal, buy a gift, write a note, or show up at a birthday party. She might mention her inability to walk but solely in the context of relearning. She never mentions being unable to read or work or take a bath or leave the house. "I'm very lucky," she says instead. Lucky? That question again. How can this be? For years,

I filed it under imponderable where it might have remained forever if not for a series of events.

One day when we were stopped at a red light on the way to my house, she turned to me. "How is your si'ter?" she asked.

Has she lost it completely, I wondered. Shocked, I had to think about my answer. Should I mention I don't have a sister?

When she'd asked where my father was twenty-five years after he died, I'd answered with a simple, "He died." This time I opted to play along. I wasn't about to bring up my brother, who was no longer living. I had never told her he died. At ninety-seven, she didn't need to know.

When the traffic signal turned green, I accelerated through the intersection. "Fine," I said, in answer to her question about my sister. "Just fine," omitting "she."

Mom nodded.

"You were a good mother," I added, shifting the topic, and reached over to pat her leg. "A very good mother."

"Tha's goo' becau' I ha'n't done anyt'ing else," she said.

It hurt that she felt that way. I longed for her to see herself differently. But this didn't seem like the time to remind her of her accomplishments. At least she hadn't shrugged off my compliment, the way she usually did. I decided right then to repeat often what a good mom she'd been. No matter that she hadn't really been my mother since I was fifteen. If she thought of herself that way, so be it.

One afternoon not long after my mother inquired about my "sister," I met a friend for coffee at a local bookstore. I informed him that something had happened to open my mind, or maybe my eyes, about my mother. "As often as I can, I tell her she's been a good mother," I said.

He leaned forward, curious.

"She has good intentions, and she's still trying to be my mom, even if her parenting gets annoying, like telling me to get my elbows off the table, brush my hair, and set the table for breakfast at night."

He laughed.

"I appreciate that she worries about me the way only mothers do. But what I don't get is why she repeats over and over that she's lucky."

"What do you *think* she means?" the friend asked.

Something in his therapeutically neutral tone of voice made me suspect he already knew the answer. But I was stymied.

"She's not referring to the past. She can't even access it much less layer it with meaning."

"So?" my friend said.

"She says she's lucky to have me. But that's not enough. She says *I'm* lucky too. Needless to say, when I'm around her, I have thoughts about how unlucky I am."

My friend leaned back in his chair.

"Her same questions over and over. Where am I? Where are we going? What day is it? And I get it. A person without a memory needs the answers. It's the repetition that makes me want to scream. Lucky? I have no idea what she's talking about. But you're looking as if you do."

"Peel the onion," my friend said. "What I think is irrelevant."

"Tell me anyway," I pleaded.

"Mull it over. Walk the dog," he said. "Let me know when you figure it out."

And so, embarrassed that I hadn't gone deeper on my own, I spent a weekend working out what my mother might mean. What I discovered was startlingly obvious.

When my mother says she's lucky, she's showing me that feeling lucky is a choice. She is showing me a way of being in the world. Choose something to feel lucky about, she's saying. Choose it in the worst of times. Find it even if nothing can be fixed. This is not easy, but she's living proof it can be done.

And when she tells me *I'm* lucky, my mother is gently reminding me to pay attention to what I often take for granted—for starters, that I can still do every single thing she has been unable to do since 1960.

Life dealt my mother and all who loved her a bad hand. Her lasting legacy to everyone who knows her has been to play it well.

It's true she hasn't made me a sandwich since I was a kid. She wasn't with me when my daughters were born. But once she got through the terrible times, she made a decision to find luck in the face of misfortune and loss. I see this clearly now and wonder how I ever could have thought I was motherless. What greater gift could a mother bestow? To the best of my ability, I now do as she does. I look for something to be thankful for.

When I reported back to my friend over another coffee, he smiled.

"To be clear," I said, "I don't feel lucky or grateful the accident happened."

"No one would," he said.

"And I'm not a believer in silver linings. Am I stronger or more courageous because of what happened? No. Has it made other losses easier? Absolutely not."

"You moved from difficult times into your changed life," he said.

"And my mother showed me how to live it. But it sure took me a long time to catch on."

"To Dorothy," he said, and lifted his cappuccino in the air.

In all honesty, I probably won't rise to the high bar my mother set. Wisps of what might have been still dim some moments, yet like cloud shadows, pass quickly by. To the good, I can usually differentiate the big stuff from the small. And I now recognize how *very* lucky I am that she's my mother, and luckily, long-lived too. I'm a hard case, and I still need her.

Chapter 28
Dorothy's Daughter

At the nursing home, my mother often hangs out in the hall-way to wait for me. When I pick her up, I notice people stop to speak to her. She nods and grins as if she understands what they are saying, though at ninety-nine, she is almost complete-ly deaf. She drools too. Her eyes don't track, and one eyelid hangs loose, exposing the scar from the surgery that was sup-posed to fix it. But her smiles and nods—and her spirit—must override how she presents.

When relatives of other residents see me with Mom, they ask if I'm Dorothy's daughter.

"I am," I say.

"I like her so much," they say, or "I really enjoy her."

"She's special," I reply, mildly astonished that strangers can see beyond her somewhat off-putting appearance.

Always a little surprised to be known as Dorothy's daugh-ter at my age, I'm also pleased. Though I may feel like a kid again, standing by, with Mom center stage, I cannot deny she still belongs there.

Lately, in my role as Dorothy's daughter, I've also become her foil, her straight man, so to speak. A month ago, I assumed she was at death's door when her aide called to report that she wasn't feeling well and had skipped a bingo game. X-rays showed double pneumonia. She stopped eating and drinking. She became dehydrated. I was worried that maybe spirit and basic good health wouldn't be enough to see her through. But she didn't even seem to be aware she was ill.

I assumed my position at her bedside. To communicate with her while she was bedridden, I resorted to a Sharpie and sketchpad. It was easier than yelling, and she had roommates.

"You are dehydrated," I printed in large block letters.

"Does'n't mean anyt'ing to me," she said, after scanning and re scanning my message.

"You need to drink more," I wrote.

"Give me whi'key," she replied.

"You have to eat too," I flashed to her.

"Wha' if I'm not hungry?" she asked.

"Your doctor says you must eat," I printed.

"Is tha' food?" she asked, pointing to the pale lumps of pureed meat and vegetables on her bed tray.

A group of staff members on their way off shift dropped by to check on her. She grinned and shook her fist at them. They laughed. She'll be fine, they told me. "And Dorothy, whenever you finally do go to heaven, please put in a good word for me," one nurse begged Mom, leaning in close to be heard. Reassured she wasn't departing for heaven quite yet, her visitors left.

"Did you go to services on Sunday?" I wrote, continuing the heaven-bound theme.

"I don' ha' to worry," she snapped.

Put in my place regarding any doubts about her ultimate destination, I continued prompting her. "Eat. You'll feel better."

"I fee' fine now. I lo'e you."

"And I love you. Can I get you anything? More water?" I asked.

"Money?" she said. "Let' go ou'."

"You have to stay in bed today."

"Why?"

"You're dehydrated. See the IV?"

"Doe'n't mean anyt'ing to me."

"Keep drinking. I love you. I want you to get well."

"I am well, I hope. You" here. I am happy."

And so it went until she pulled out her IV and started drinking and eating with gusto again, roaming the halls, picking up trash, turning off lights, playing cards and bingo and going to programs or on outings with Don and me. "She's back," the staff reported when she resumed ordering them to water the potted plant above the drinking fountain. But not forever.

Almost seventy years is a long time to have a mother. Anyone would think me greedy if I said I want even more time, yet I need a few more years, and she never mentions being ready to leave, so I'm planning her hundredth birthday party. "For me?" she says, shaking her head in disbelief.

I'm sure that along with devastating loss, I'll feel some sense of relief when she goes, and I am no longer responsible for her. But for now and as always, she exceeds all expectations at finding joy. I hope she'll be up for a card game until the moment she takes her last breath but accept that our rituals—ever more precious—will change. Just not yet.

"Time to go, Mom," I say on Sunday after she beats me at Crazy Eights.

"Hurry! Le's go befo' they lock the door," she says, rolling herself back from the table.

"They won't lock you out," I reassure her. "Ready?"

An aide meets us at the door of the nursing home. "Love you, Mom," I say, and wave. "Stay out of trouble."

"Impossib'," she says.

As the aide starts to push my mother down the hall, she puts her foot down to brake.

"Kath'een," she calls. "Don' go." She looks up at me and repeats the farewell she spoke when leaving the ER after she broke her leg—a perfect epitaph if ever she needs one.

"Goo'bye. Than' you. I ha' a won'erfu' time."

Epilogue

My mother died at age ninety-nine. On the last day of her life, she and I played Crazy Eights after which she attended her weekly bingo game. Skipping lunch, she went directly to bed for her afternoon nap. I crawled in bed with her for a while and then left for home. Her last words were, "I love you."

The Call came at midnight. An hour later, she slipped quietly away, Don and I at her side.

CPSIA information can be obtained
at www.ICGtesting.com
Printed in the USA
JSHW012043091122
32907JS00001BA/11